Twayne's United States Authors Series

Sylvia E. Bowman, *Editor*

INDIANA UNIVERSITY

Burton Rascoe

BURTON RASCOE

By DONALD M. HENSLEY
Wagner College

Twayne Publishers, Inc.   ::   New York

For Joyce

Acknowledgments

I would like to express my gratitude to the following for permission to quote from letters and from copyrighted material:

To Sculley Bradley for permission to quote from his review of *Prometheans*, "Rascoe Makes Literature a Living Subject," which appeared in the *Philadelphia Record*, December 17, 1933.

To Margaret Freeman Cabell for permision to quote from the letters of James Branch Cabell to Rascoe in the Burton Rascoe Collection.

To the *Chicago Tribune* for permission to quote from Rascoe's article, "Some Impressions of Hergesheimer and of 'Java Head,'" March 8, 1919, books sec., p. 9.

To Doubleday and Company, Inc., for permission to reprint the drawing of Rascoe from the dust jacket of Rascoe's *We Were Interrupted*. Copyright 1947 by Burton Rascoe.

To Doubleday and Company, Inc., for permission to quote from "On a Certain Condescension in Our Natives," "Our Vicious Zeal," "Prof. Sherman Gives Asylum to His Brood," and "Carl Sandburg," from Rascoe's *Before I Forget*. Copyright 1937 by Burton Rascoe. Copyright 1918 by the *Chicago Tribune*. Copyright 1924 by the *New York Evening Post*.

To Lewis Galantière for permission to quote from his letters to Rascoe in the Rascoe Collection.

To the *New York Sun* for permission to quote from Rascoe's column, "A Bookman's Daybook," July 16, 1932, p. 16, in which Rascoe reviewed Grant C. Knight's *American Literature and Culture*.

To Louis Paul for permission to quote from his letters to Rascoe in the Rascoe Collection and from his article, "Books and Mr. Rascoe," *Reading and Collecting: A Monthly Review of Rare and Recent Books*, I (May, 1937), 15, 29. Also I would like to make separate acknowledgment to Mr. Paul for making a selection of Rascoe's letters to him available to me.

To the *Richmond Times-Dispatch* for permission to quote from Alan Burton Clarke's review, "Mr. Rascoe and Some Other Titans of Literature," November 27, 1932, sec. III, p. 4.

To Edmund Wilson for permission to quote from one of his letters in the Rascoe Collection.

Preface

BURTON RASCOE'S writings are still mentioned sometimes by literary biographers and by literary historians of the 1910's and 1920's (he is never mentioned in the more formalistic criticism); but for the most part he is by now either forgotten or —at best—dismissed as having merely historical importance. This neglect is not surprising, however, to anyone who knows literary history. Even major writers are sometimes forgotten; so it is hardly surprising when someone of Rascoe's stature seems to be headed—undeservedly or not—for oblivion.

Actually, as this study attempts to show, Rascoe exerted a considerable influence on the literary life of his times. As a critic, he exposed much of the artificiality of the literature and fought for a distinctive American literature and language: he fought against the "genteel" tradition, academicism and pedantry, the literary humanists, censorship, and the control of American literature by foreign literature and writers. He played a useful role in contributing to the public acceptance of H. L. Mencken, Theodore Dreiser, T. S. Eliot, Sherwood Anderson, Ernest Hemingway, James Branch Cabell, Edmund Wilson, and many others; and he was important as a publicizer of their work. He provided significant personal and professional help to many young writers; and, as an editor, he inspired them to do their best work, provided opportunities for them, and helped establish their reputations. In his efforts to democratize American literature and culture, he did some of the important early work in helping to broaden, to enlarge, and to raise America's culture standards and literary level; and he is a writer whose importance and influence are still underestimated.

Rascoe's neglect was not always the case. From the decade before 1920 and through the 1920's he had a reputation as an *avant-garde* critic and editor. But by the mid-1930's changes in literary fashions and critical assumptions, as well as political and economic developments, had begun to dim his reputation; but he still had defenders. In the late 1940's and 1950's he was nearly forgotten. Chapter 4 of this study outlines Rascoe's changing reputation and reception as a critic.

The introductory chapter intends to show Rascoe the man and his work. This chapter traces his development as a literary critic and editor, and relates the main events of his career to his times. The emphasis is on presenting new information and in correcting misinformation—some of which Rascoe himself helped to perpetrate.

Chapter 2 summarizes Rascoe's principal critical theories and describes and illustrates his style and personal methods of criticism. Chapter 3 discusses in more detail some representative examples of his work as a critic and editor from 1917 until 1932, his most productive years. In this chapter, as in the others, I have decided to let Rascoe speak for himself since I am quoting from uncollected works. None of his books is still in print, and very little of his work—some of it among his best—which appeared in various newspapers, magazines, and journals has ever been reprinted. Therefore, I felt that a discussion of Rascoe's work would be ineffective unless some attempts were made to show also the quality of his mind and art. The final chapter lists some of Rascoe's considerable contributions to the development of American literary life and attempts to fix his significance in literary history.

A study of this sort would not have been possible a few years ago. It is possible now only because of the availability of new source material in the Burton Rascoe Collection in the Library of the University of Pennsylvania. This rich collection contains Rascoe's correspondence, his scrapbooks of clippings by and about him, his early diaries and journals, typescripts and manuscripts of his articles and books (many of them unpublished), his library, and copies of the extensive Rascoe-to-James Branch Cabell correspondence (owned by the Alderman Library of the University of Virginia). The Rascoe-to-Cabell correspondence is the best—and in many cases the only—source for verifying actual events and activities in Rascoe's career.

This study relies mainly on these new materials, particularly on the correspondence; limited use has been made of the often unreliable material found in Rascoe's impressionistic two-volume autobiography, *Before I Forget* (1937) and *We Were Interrupted* (1947), although these two books should be consulted for more detailed biographical data.

My greatest debt in doing *Burton Rascoe* is to Mrs. Burton

Rascoe for her permission to use and quote from the works of Burton Rascoe, including his correspondence, unpublished manuscripts, and published works to which she holds the copyright, all of which are in the Rascoe Collection. I am most grateful to her. I am also grateful to the Curator of the Rare Book Collection of the University of Pennsylvania, Mrs. Neda M. Westlake, for permission to use and quote from the materials in the Rascoe Collection which are under the University of Pennsylvania's control. I wish also to express here my gratitude to Mrs. Westlake and her staff for the generous amount of time and effort they spent in making these materials available to me. My other debts I acknowledge separately.

DONALD M. HENSLEY

Staten Island, New York

Contents

Chronology

1892   October 22, (Arthur) Burton Rascoe born Fulton, Kentucky; oldest of three sons of Matthew Lafayette and Elizabeth Burton Rascoe.

1903   Family moves to Shawnee, Oklahoma.

1908   At sixteen Rascoe becomes reporter and editorial writer for the *Shawnee Herald,* and assistant librarian of the Carnegie Public Library in Shawnee.

1911   Graduates from Shawnee High School. In August goes to Chicago. October 1, enters the University of Chicago. Does odd jobs in Chicago to support self; becomes campus correspondent for the Chicago newspaper *Inter-Ocean.*

1912   January, becomes campus correspondent for the *Chicago Tribune.* Is a regular reporter on the staff of the *Tribune* from June until October 1. October, starts second year at the University of Chicago; continues as campus correspondent for the *Tribune.* Fall, writes first book reviews for the *Tribune.*

1913   June, at end of school year, withdraws from the university and resumes job as reporter on the regular staff of the *Tribune.* July 5, marries Hazel Luke in Chicago.

1914   Arthur Burton, Jr., born July 2.

1916   Becomes chief book reviewer of the *Tribune.*

1917   Fall, begins Chicago literary battles for H. L. Mencken and James Branch Cabell.

1918   Ruth Helen Rascoe born January 30. February, becomes literary editor of the *Chicago Tribune.* Attacks Ben Hecht, Rupert Hughes, Keith Preston, Conrad Aiken, Lewis Galantière in his defense of Cabell.

1919–   Writes introductions for four books in Knopf's Borzoi series
1923   of French classics: Flaubert's *Madame Bovary* (1919), Abbé Prévost's *Manon Lescaut* (1919), Gautier's *Mademoiselle de Maupin* (1920), Zola's *Nana* (1922). Writes introductions for three books in the Modern Library series: Ben Hecht's *Erik Dorn* (1921), Cabell's *Chivalry* (1922), and Gabriel D'Annunzio's *The Triumph of Death* (1923).

1920 May, fired by the *Chicago Tribune*. Goes to Seminole, Oklahoma, and for seven months lives and works on a farm, reads, and does freelance work.

1921 January until May, manages and writes for the Chicago Bureau of the Newspaper Enterprise Association. April until March, 1922, associate editor of *McCall's* in New York City.

1922 March 4, publishes "Notes for an Epitaph: H. L. Mencken" in The Literary Review of the *New York Evening Post*.

1922– April 1, through August, 1924, literary editor of the *New*
1924 *York Tribune* (later—in 1924—the *Herald Tribune*). Publishes popular diary-like column, "A Bookman's Day Book," in the *New York Tribune* from April, 1922, through August, 1924.

1924 August 31, fired by *New York Herald Tribune*. March, becomes literary critic for *Arts and Decoration*, until 1932. Becomes literary critic for the *Detroit Athletic Club News*, until 1948. November through December, in Paris.

1925 January 1 through September, 1927, assistant feature editor of Johnson Features (of Editors Features Service), and writes syndicated daily column, "The Daybook of a New Yorker," appearing in three hundred and fifty to four hundred newspapers. Rascoe's first book—and the first book on Dreiser—is published: *Theodore Dreiser*.

1926 August until September, 1927, writes weekly book reviews for Johnson Features, appearing in over sixty newspapers.

1927 September through April, 1928, editor and critic, *The Bookman*. Becomes editor on Board of Editors of The Literary Guild of America, until May, 1937 .

1928– Edits and writes calendars and horoscopes for *Morrow's*
1930 *Almanack;* does same for 1929; and writes introductory essays for all of the months of the *Almanack* for 1930.

1929 August through June, 1930, associate editor and critic, *Plain Talk* magazine. Rascoe's *A Bookman's Daybook* published, edited by C. Hartley Grattan.

1930 February until December, editorial adviser for the Robert M. McBride publishing company. Attacks the New Humanists in articles in the *New York World, Plain Talk*, and in

"Pupils of Polonius" in *The Critique of Humanism* (ed. Grattan).

1931 June until July, 1933, literary critic for the *New York Sun*.

1932 February through October, writes *Titans of Literature*, published November 1. December until April, 1938, literary critic for *Esquire*. Writes first strong attacks on communism and pro-communist writers, to continue through the 1930's and 1940's.

1933 March through October, writes *Prometheans*.

1934 Spring until May, 1937, general editorial adviser for Doubleday, Doran and Company. Writes the history of *The Smart Set* magazine and edits (with Groff Conklin) *The Smart Set Anthology*.

1936 Burton Rascoe, Jr., twenty-two, takes own life, September 19.

1937 Writes *Before I Forget, The Joys of Reading*, and the Introduction to Oscar Wilde's *The Ballad of Reading Gaol* (Limited Editions Club). May, resigns as editorial adviser to Doubleday, Doran and as editor-in-chief of the Literary Guild. Is sued for $250,000 by Max Annenberg for material about Annenberg in *Before I Forget*.

1938 April 25 until September 11, 1939, book reviewer for *Newsweek* magazine. Edits *An American Reader* for G. P. Putnam's Sons, published September. Expresses strong anti-British feelings in 1938 and 1939; thinks Britain conniving with Germany. Is hospitalized three days from overwork. Takes Caribbean cruise: to Panama, Columbia, Venezuela, Haiti.

1939 March through September, writes New York column, "Burton Rascoe Says," for the Shawnee, Oklahoma, News Company. Writes Introduction for Dreiser's *Sister Carrie* (Limited Editions Club). May, in hospital for nervous breakdown. In Oklahoma, November until December 24, working on novel, *The Boomer*.

1940 Literary critic for *The American Mercury* magazine. Is desperate for writing jobs, until late in 1942. Sells his rare books and first editions.

1941 Publishes *Belle Starr: "The Bandit Queen"*. Takes job writing column for new *Chicago Sun*, until June 1, 1942.

1942 October 20 until April 4, 1946, drama critic for the *New York World-Telegram*.

1947 Publishes *We Were Interrupted*. Writes articles for *Plain Talk, The American Weekly* (Hearst Sunday Supplement), *True, Today's Woman, The Encyclopedia Americana, The Encyclopedia Britannica*.

1948 October until April, 1949, directs Playwrights Educational Theatre, Adelphi College, Garden City, New York.

1949– Freelancing and doing editorial work: writes for *The Free-*
1954 *man, The American Legion Magazine, Human Events;* does editorial work and writes introductions for Avon Publications and for Gold Medal Books.

1954 April 20 until March 18, 1957, writes syndicated newspaper column, "TV First-Nighter," for Classic Features.

1957 March 19 dies, New York City. April 24, University of Pennsylvania acquires the Burton Rascoe Collection.

CHAPTER *1*

Life, Times, and Controversies

IN THE SMALL, caste-ridden Southern town of Fulton, Kentucky, located in the southwest corner of the state near the Tennessee state line, Burton Rascoe was born on October 22, 1892, the first of three sons of Matthew Lafayette and Elizabeth Burton Rascoe. There he spent the first eleven years of his childhood. He has written about his life in Fulton in his autobiography, *Before I Forget*,[1] and in his unpublished autobiographical novel, *Gustibus*;[2] in these works he relates his memories and impressions of events and experiences in these first years. A precocious child, he was happy learning about nature, going to school, or just being alone with his father. But, coming from a poor family, he was often made unhappy, for he felt the inevitable pain inherent in the caste system.

Yet on that icy winter day in 1903 when his family moved to Shawnee, Oklahoma, where his father had been offered a job managing a hotel restaurant and bar, he felt completely disoriented. However, he adjusted to the move and the new surroundings easily and quickly, as children usually do. Shawnee was another small town, but Rascoe found it more exciting and democratic than moribund Fulton. Oklahoma, not even a state in 1903, still had many frontier characteristics; these were to help shape Rascoe's distinctive personality, tastes, attitudes, and points of view. He lived in Shawnee until he was nearly nineteen.

Contributing equally to the development of Rascoe's character during these highly formative years was his relationship with his parents. His mother and father had come from different social levels—his mother had defied her prosperous father and had eloped with Rascoe's father, who had been a hired hand on the Burton farm. One consequence of this difference was that Rascoe's father had no trouble adapting to the frontier conditions of Oklahoma, but his mother resisted the change and resented the crude, "vulgar" way of life there. In Chapter Two of *Before I Forget*, Rascoe has described his mother as being cold and emotionless, contrasting her with his warm and emotional father. Rascoe always wrote admiringly of his father, with warm praise for his father's natural abilities and achievements; but for his puritanical mother he developed ambivalent feelings of affection and distaste which he finally resolved by finding ways of "escaping" from her.

I *The Reader*

Rascoe's intellectual life dates from the time he entered high school, when he was fourteen and became interested in literature. He wrote essays in his English notebook on Victor Hugo, William Cullen Bryant, Robert Louis Stevenson, Edgar Allan Poe, and Thomas Carlyle.[3] And he kept diaries and journals (imitating Emerson) in 1909 and 1910 that show that he was reading widely. This early reading he listed in *Before I Forget*, a list of titles that came to several pages.[4] His diaries and journals show that he was also planning to become a writer. He noted in his diary on January 19, 1909, that "I wrote an article for the [Shawnee] Herald on Poe and was agreeably surprised to learn that it would be placed in the editorial column." On January 22 he wrote that "it is my desire to know all the interesting men that it is possible for me to meet."

Over and over again he stated his desire to own a big library some day. On February 7, 1909, he wrote: "If I were to steal I should steal books; if any one ever steals from me I would rather he take anything or things other than my books. My dreams are of a vast library." He announced his future plans as a writer in his journal; about Whitman he wrote: "Fifty years hence he will be appreciated. I shall help to make him so."[5] And about the drama: "The stage has become a radical pulpit, the play a preachment. I am going to strive to bring the drama back to an art."[6]

In literature Rascoe had found an escape from the harsher aspects of unsettled frontier life in Shawnee as well as from the hurt that came from the bickerings of a poor family with divided aims. With the help of literature, he was determined to find value and meaning within himself. As a consequence, he became extremely self-reliant. For example, when his parents moved to Seminole, a little town a few miles southeast of Shawnee, he remained in Shawnee to finish high school. He supported himself by working for the local newspaper, by working in the Carnegie Public Library in Shawnee, and by writing literary papers for members of the various local women's clubs.[7] In his junior year in high school Rascoe wrote his first of many newspaper columns. Written for the *Shawnee Herald*, it was called "Séances with the Mental Medium: Reports of Visits Made by Burton Rascoe." In this column Rascoe invented a retired professor and recorded his sayings. Rascoe did so, he said, because he doubted people would be interested in what a sixteen-year-old boy had to say.[8]

II *Chicago—College*

In 1911, when Rascoe finished high school, he planned to attend the University of Chicago. He knew that he would have to work his way through college, just as he had through high school, but he was prepared to do so; and so he left Shawnee in August to go to Chicago to find a job before starting school on October 1. When school started, he enrolled at the university; he also took a job as campus correspondent for the Chicago newspaper *Inter-Ocean*. He had nearly perfect qualifications even then for newspaper work: he was resourceful, independent, courageous, ambitious, and he could write readable copy quickly about almost any topic.

It was not long before he discovered that the journals published by university presses were excellent sources for news stories. He wrote later that he recognized that these journals "quite frequently contain something not only news but downright startling and of interest to the ordinary newspaper reader. The authors, however, have no sense of the news value of their discoveries. . . . I made it my business to read these stodgy journals with close attention. I often got first-page news stories out of them."[9] Thus he early became a kind of popularizer of other men's work, and this work was to continue to be one of his most important contributions to the developing American culture before and during the 1920's and in the 1930's. But in 1912 his ability to use such sources landed him a part-time job with the *Chicago Tribune;* he was hired because the *Tribune* liked a story he wrote about cheating and stealing among high school students, the facts of which he had taken from *The American Journal of Sociology.*[10]

Between his freshman and sophomore year—from June until October—Rascoe worked full time for the *Tribune*. And at the end of his sophomore year (in 1913), he decided to leave the university to go to work full-time for the *Tribune*. He said in *Before I Forget* that he had made this decision because he was completely disillusioned with the kind of education he was getting at the university.[11] It is more likely, however, that the reason was in part that he had never felt as if he "belonged" at the university; he reacted to this hurt by rejecting that university which he felt had rejected him. This feeling of not fully belonging to anyone or anything was to haunt Rascoe throughout his life and to result in a pattern of ambivalent feelings toward his parents (perhaps the source of it all), toward the University of Chicago, toward his friends and family, and toward his numerous jobs. Alfred Kazin was later to write (correctly, I think) that Rascoe even felt this way about literature—that he always felt that he was on the outside looking in at writers instead of being a writer (which he was) on the inside looking out.[12] This fear of rejection, and feeling of alienation, is reflected in the careers he selected for himself and what he made of them. It is perhaps significant that Rascoe, for all his attacks on academic critics and college professors, tried to get the University of Chicago to award him an honorary degree. Howard P. Hudson, associate editor of *The University of Chicago Magazine,* told Rascoe in a letter on July 10, 1939, that he did "not believe President Hutchins would consider any of my recommendations for candidates for honorary degrees. And if those are your terms [for Rascoe's writing an article on his experiences at the University of Chicago for the magazine] I'm afraid it's a stalemate."

Having apparently decided on a career as a newspaperman, and having a full-time job with the *Chicago Tribune,* Rascoe felt that he had security enough to get married. On July 5, 1913, he and Hazel Luke were married in Chicago. Nearly a year later, on July 2, 1914, their son, Burton, Jr., was born. In the next few years Rascoe held a variety of writing and editorial jobs on the *Tribune.* Then in 1916 Mrs. Elia W. Peattie moved to New York to be near her son, Donald Culross Peattie; and Rascoe was made the chief book reviewer. In February, 1918, at the retirement of Robert Burns Peattie and Mrs. Peattie, he became literary editor.[13]

III   *The Battle for American Writers*

Rascoe's most important work in Chicago began in 1917 and continued until 1920. He has described his work in *Before I Forget*: "Being literary editor, writing of books, staging fights among the literati, hailing meritorious new authors, stirring up the intellectuals, attacking censorship, fighting what I believed to be the good fight for life and literature—that was what pleased me most then; that was what I considered true fun."[14]

In whatever way he could, Rascoe opened the *Tribune* book pages to the new spirit expressing itself in modern literature which, he felt, came closer to expressing the truth of the conditions of the times. In his own book reviews, literary essays, and editorials, and in the book pages which he edited, he fearlessly assailed the old and championed the new. Bernard Duffey in his *The Chicago Renaissance in American Letters: A Critical History* praises Rascoe for opening "full the gates of the *Tribune* to Chicago's renaissance." Rascoe, Duffey says, "more strictly perhaps than any of his contemporaries . . . argued the cause and forwarded the accomplishments of the early Liberation."[15] His friend Lewis Galantière recalled in a letter of April 7, 1919, to Rascoe that aspect of Rascoe's work: "Then [a year earlier—in 1918] we both enjoyed the sight on the printed page of 'pimp' and 'strumpet' and other such words merely as an expression of defiance to convention, to stilted 'classical' writing."

We can see now that this courageous defiance characterized his book pages on the *Tribune*. For example, in a review which appeared in the *Tribune* on April 1, 1916, he praised Willard Huntington Wright's Nietzschean novel, *The Man of Promise*, writing in part: "No drivel here; no sop to the catharists; a straight-forward, conscientious, and supremely artistic effort to lift our American fiction above the fifth rate place it occupies in the world of letters. . . ."[16] In a letter to Rascoe, Wright expressed his gratitude for Rascoe's "bravery in praising my novel."[17] In 1920, Wright wrote again to say to Rascoe—ironically, just a month before Rascoe was fired by the *Chicago Tribune*—that he thought that Rascoe's "work on the *Tribune* is what we've all been waiting and hoping for."[18]

Like most Americans literarily aware in this period, Rascoe recognized and admired the new work coming from Europe. He later proudly recalled in *We Were Interrupted* having read and written about Proust's *Remembrance of Things Past* (first two sections): "this was four years before Proust was translated into English and five years before a book of tributes to Proust was issued . . ."; he also remembered "touting W. Somerset Maugham's *Of Human Bondage* and Norman Douglas's *South Wind* eight years before these books were 'discovered' and touted . . . in New York. . . ."[19] However, despite this appeal of the European writers and culture—the modern French writers especially appealed to him[20]—Rascoe decided to go to war for an American literature as indigenous as possible. In a letter to Cabell about Theodore Dreiser's work, he explained his position:

> I haven't read "Jenny Gerhardt" since I first read it, several years ago—a severe criticism in itself probably—but I remember that I was considerably impressed with the novel; and, with the exception of "The 'Genius' " and the volume of short stories called "Free," I have always honored Dreiser's sincerity, his lumbering efforts at truthful portrayal, his fidelity to his middle-class viewpoint of middle-class life, and his honest reflection of phases of American life. I know well enough that Dreiser can hardly write a decent sentence, that, at times, he is grotesquely sentimental, and that he has an absurd idea that he is a philosopher; but with all that he has courage, a valuable ability at documentation, an intellectual honesty, and an inquisitive mind, always seeking to learn everything he can about people, their queer twists, their ideas about life, their reasons for doing this and that. If this aim and intention is praiseworthy in Englishmen and in Frenchmen, it is praiseworthy in an American. We haven't a Hardy or a Balzac, a Chekhov, a Mann, a Barbusse, a Bennett, a Charles-Louis Phillipe unless we count Dreiser and Sherwood Anderson. Both of them do somewhat the same for America that these fellows have done for their milieu. So, whatever be the ultimate value of such intention, it should [be] appraised, I think, with the intention in mind.[21]

Though it was not apparent at first, Rascoe planned his Chicago literary battles; for the recognition of contemporary American writers—Sherwood Anderson, Dreiser, Carl Sandburg, Henry Blake Fuller, H. L. Mencken, James Branch Cabell, and many others—he made controversy his business. He attacked these writers' enemies, exhorted his readers to read their works, and even—when he could get away with it—printed their work for pay. Furthermore, he encouraged them in an enormous correspondence. Nevertheless, the *Chicago Tribune* fired Rascoe in early May, 1920, because, as he explained in *Before I Forget*, he had referred lightly to the Christian Scientists. A powerful economic group in Chicago, they had threatened to boycott the *Tribune's* business office if Rascoe were not fired.[22] Mencken wrote to him on May 6 to congratulate him on his "escape";[23] and the next day George Jean Nathan wrote to Rascoe and asked him to come to New York.[24] But Rascoe, who would be twenty-eight in October, had been working under constant nervous tension and pressure for the past eight years; he decided, therefore, that he needed a long, health-bringing rest. He took his family, along with a plentiful supply of books, and went to live on his parents' farm in Seminole, Oklahoma. There he lived for the remainder of 1920.

Rascoe had never earned much money while working for the *Chicago Tribune*. His total income for the four months that he worked there in 1920 was $2,635, but of this only $1,530 had been salary; he had earned $1,105 from his other writings. In 1919 his total income had been $4,618.10.[25] But in this new decade, though it began with him out of a job, he earned more money than he had ever earned before or would ever earn afterward. He told Percy Hammond that in 1925 his salary was ten thousand dollars, and that in addition he had earned $6,478.90 from stocks.[26] Later in the 1920's his earnings—particularly those from stocks—went even higher; but they dropped just as drastically in the 1930's. He wrote to his mother on June 10, 1932, that the previous week he had earned thirty-five dollars, that the week before that he had earned thirty-four dollars, and that he had less than fifty dollars in the bank.[27]

IV *Editor and Critic*

In January, 1921, after nearly eight months of rest, Rascoe moved back into his old apartment at 1433 Sherwin Street, Chicago. He had turned down an editorial job with the Newspaper Enterprise Association (NEA), but he had agreed to write for and to manage NEA's Chicago Bureau. A few months later, however, he was asked by Harry Payne Burton to come to New York as an associate editor of *McCall's;* he accepted Burton's offer and began work at *McCall's* on April 1.[28]

He was conscientious enough about his editorial duties at *McCall's*, which he has described fully in *We Were Interrupted;* but he also found time to write "critical essays, articles, personality sketches, and book reviews [for] the *New Republic*, the *Nation*, the *Reviewer*, the *Bookman*, the *New Freeman*, the *Double-Dealer* (a little *Tendenz* magazine then published in New Orleans and edited by John McClure, a poet), the Literary Review of the New York *Evening Post*, and the New York *Tribune*." His writings while at *McCall's* included "... essays on George Santayana, Max Beerbohm, Stendhal, Clive Bell, Emile Zola, Rémy de Gourmont, Théophile Gautier, the poetry of Conrad Aiken, character studies of Sherwood Anderson, H. L. Mencken, Joseph Hergesheimer, Henry Blake Fuller, and Carl Sandburg; on the biblical style; on farmers and bank loans in Oklahoma; and reviews of many current books; a short story for the *Smart Set*, and a piece in the *Bookman* that caused a great deal of consternation among motion-picture producers and distributors. It was called 'The Motion Pictures: An Industry, Not an Art.' "[29]

On March 1, 1922, Rascoe left *McCall's* to become literary editor of the *New York Tribune*. Since his first task was to organize a staff, he hired Lewis Galantière, now living in Paris, to write "a weekly letter ... of news and comment on the new books and literary affairs in France";[30] Douglas Goldring, in London, to write an English letter; and Ernest Boyd, in New York, to write about books "from Ireland, Italy, Germany, Spain, and the Scandinavian countries."[31] He appointed a staff of regular reviewers —"Will Cuppy, Ben Ray Redman, Bruce Gould, A. Donald Douglas, Howard Irving Young, Stanton Coblentz, and Isabel Patterson"; and he was soon getting special reviews from "Elinor Wylie, Thomas Beer, Henry Blake Fuller, Paul Shorey, Edmund Wilson, Gilbert Seldes, Nicholas Roosevelt, Ben Hecht, Zelda Fitzgerald, and Carl Van Vechten."[32]

He announced his plans in his first issue; and it is easy to see in retrospect that he planned no changes from what he had done in Chicago—he would continue to write subjective criticism, to attack blind academic critics, and to fight for American literature and writers.[33] He did start something new, however, in his second issue: he began his diary-like column, "A Bookman's Day Book," which he continued to write until he left the *Tribune* nearly two and one-half years later.[34] But about this column he said to

Cabell: "The diary is a damned nuisance. The first one I wrote largely as a joke and to show up the other personality columns. Tried to kill it then by attributing a disparaging remark about the thing to the managing editor. But it was greeted enthusiastically and the people here, as well as those I see, don't want me to quit it. When I write anything else, no one ever comments upon that but always on the diary. I am doomed to be a clown."[35] Yet in *We Were Interrupted* he pointed out that in the "Day Book" ". . . I could record briefly my impressions of many books which interested me to which I could not devote space in formal reviews."[36]

That Rascoe's work was being followed is easily shown; one of his readers was Ernest Hemingway, who wrote in 1923 in a letter to Edmund Wilson about criticism in America that "Rascoe was intelligent about Eliot."[37] Harry Hansen later wrote Rascoe that "I *know* how your Daybook was read. It was the sensation of its day."[38] Nevertheless, on June 5, 1924, Rascoe informed Cabell that he was being fired by the *Herald-Tribune* (the *Tribune* and the *Herald* had merged on March 19, 1924) and that Stuart P. Sherman would replace him as literary editor. Rascoe was allowed to stay with the paper through August, however, which he was forced to do because he needed the money.

Edmund Wilson's anonymous article, "The All-Star Literary Vaudeville," which appeared in *The New Republic* on June 30, 1926, and which he included in 1956 in *A Literary Chronicle: 1920–1950*, contained Wilson's opinion about Rascoe's work on the *Tribune;* and he also implied the reason for Rascoe's being fired:

Burton Rascoe has performed the astonishing and probably unprecedented feat of making literature into news. A master of all the tricks of newspaper journalism, which he has introduced into the Sacred Grove to the horror of some of its high priests, his career has been singularly honorable in its disregard of popular values; and the cause of letters has profited more from his activities than the proprietors of popular newspapers who have inevitably discovered in the long run that they would feel more comfortable with a literary editor who did not find books so exciting. Mr. Rascoe has always written respectably and, at his best, with much ease and point.[39]

V   *Editor and Columnist*

To Cabell, Rascoe wrote on October 21, 1924, that he was going to Europe for about eight weeks, and would return on January 1 to a well-paying job. Harry Payne Burton, editor of *McCall's*, wrote to Rascoe in Paris on November 18, 1924, saying that he had heard about Rascoe's new job with Johnson Features, which was to begin the first of the year at a salary of about twelve thousand dollars. When Rascoe and his wife visited Paris in November and December, they met Hemingway, E. E. Cummings, and their old friend, Lewis Galantière. When Rascoe was interviewed about French literature by Victor Llona for *Le Journal Littéraire*, Rascoe discussed contemporary French influences on American writers and on himself; and he evinced an awareness of French writers that were then still untranslated into English:

> Verlaine, Corbière, Laforgue, Rimbaud and even Mallarmé un-
> questionably influenced our young poets. T. S. Eliot can be said
> to have been influenced by Laforgue and by Corbière, as was
> E. E. Cummings by Verlaine and by Rimbaud.
> . . . .
> Personally, I was much influenced by Rémy de Gourmont. This
> great writer touches us greatly by a mysticism mixed with scien-
> tific tendencies against which, however, we should energetically
> defend ourselves, for we are only too inclined to abandon our-
> selves to it. The influence of Barrès is negligible. He has not been
> translated into our language. Moreover, we already have enough
> apologists for imposed order, and his esthetic teachings would,
> I fear, escape us.
> Now that [Anatole] France is dead, I believe that one could
> say, without fear of contradiction, that André Gide incontestably
> occupies first place in the forefront of your best writers. Among
> us he is known and greatly appreciated by an elite. I am happy
> that it has finally been decided to translate him. He will thus
> penetrate very deeply in our country. *Straight Is the Gate* touches
> the Puritan conscience to the quick.[40]

When Rascoe returned to the United States, he began work on January 1, 1925, as an associate feature editor and syndicated columnist for the newspaper syndicate, Editors Features Service. He wrote a daily column, the "Day Book of a New Yorker," in which he gave his observations and impressions of life in New York. This column appeared in from three hundred and fifty to four hundred newspapers, and it ran for nearly three years—until September, 1927. In August, 1926, Rascoe also began writing weekly a "Book Revue" column for Editors Features Service (but distributed through Johnson Features, Inc.), and it was syndicated in sixty-four newspapers. On September 13, 1927, V. V. McNitt, president and general manager of Editors Features Service, wrote to Rascoe to try to persuade him to continue his "Day Book" column, but Rascoe refused. Leslie P. Eichel, editor of Editors Features Service, wrote the next day (September 14) for the same reason, but by that time Rascoe was already editing *The Bookman,* his first issue being the September, 1927, issue.

VI *His Life's Work*

In 1926 Rascoe alluded, in a letter to Dreiser about *An American Tragedy* and its critical reception, to his own ambitions and plans:

> I cannot tell you how much your serious talk with me yesterday morning helped to clarify many of my problems, gave me renewed assurance and set me up in every way. I love you with a great and deep affection, and I admire you more than any man I have ever met. I was flattered and made happy to know that you took an interest in me and that you sensed that I have not only potentialities but a program and also that you feel what my egoism conceals from most people and that is this: that I know in my heart that ultimately I shall have my say and make my mark upon the thought of our times.[41]

From this letter to Dreiser, and from another to Rascoe a month later from Lewis Galantière in Paris, we can infer that Rascoe was thinking about spending more time on his novel, *Gustibus,* on which he had been working sporadically for years. Galantière in his letter said to Rascoe: "You are ... a man with a mercurial mind, an inquisitive intelligence; you are a champion of ideas, not a creator of worlds or people. I haven't seen your novel, but I'll bet a hat it is satirical and analytical; that you expose and exploit foibles more than you create character or situation even. You can never abandon your interest in what the world is thinking and writing from month to month...."[42] Galantière was right; Rascoe was never able to finish the novel, even though it was announced in a publisher's catalogue; and years later he was able to use to use most of it in his autobiography, *Before I Forget,* without making many changes.

Additional confirmation of Galantière's opinion appeared a year later in "A Salute to Youth," which Rascoe wrote for the Celebrities Number of *The Daily Maroon,* the student magazine of the University of Chicago. Written as Rascoe was approaching his thirty-fifth birthday, he said in it:

> Like all men of my age, I have a notion that my life's work is yet before me. I nourish the belief that in time I shall do great and worthy things. I am growing mellow and "mature"; my opinions are settling into convictions; my prejudices are tending toward the standard. People . . . are beginning to look upon me as a man of judgment, serenity of mind, disciplined emotions, and capacity for thought.
>
> Certainly my capacity to respond to external stimuli—the stimuli of music, of painting, of literature, of persons, of things, is not so great as it was when I was twenty-five. My capacity for wonder, for hope, for pleasure, for fighting for the things I believe in, has appreciably decreased during the past ten years. I do not get excited about ideas as I once did. I am beginning to find more pleasure in the manner by which a thing is accomplished than in the thing itself. More likely to understand without enjoying a symphony, more able to define with some exactitude the pleasure experienced at the sight of a piece of sculpture, more likely to marvel more at the method by which Proust recreates a scene than at the scene itself.[43]

In April, 1927, while still writing his syndicated columns for Johnson Features, Rascoe wrote to Cabell that he had agreed to edit *Morrow's Almanack* for 1928; and he asked Cabell if he would contribute an article.[44] Rascoe edited the *Almanack* for 1928 and 1929, writing the bogus horoscopes and compiling the calendars; but, because he had hardly made expenses out of it in 1928 and 1929, he refused to edit the *Almanack* for 1930, although he did write short essays for each month of that year's *Almanack.*

When his friend Seward Collins purchased *The Bookman* in 1927, Rascoe, who by then had a reputation as a successful editor, was asked to edit the magazine. Rascoe accepted, and that summer he worked on *The Bookman,* the *Almanack,* and—until September—for Johnson Features. His first issue of *The Bookman* in

September contained contributions by Cabell, Dreiser, Liam O'Flaherty, Upton Sinclair, Keith Preston, E. E. Cummings, Gilbert Seldes, Hugh Walpole, John Farrar, Dorothy Parker, John Macy, and Rascoe himself. On September 8, Rascoe wrote to thank Dreiser for his contribution: "Here is a check for 'Portrait of a Woman.' Thanks very much for letting me have the sketch. It contributed vastly to the success of my first number, and I am grateful to you." He then asked Dreiser for two more articles.[45] Years later Rascoe wrote to David Smart, publisher of *Esquire,* that "'The Bookman'. . . jumped from 7,000 to over 40,000 with the first issue under my editorship and climbed to over 60,000 with the next issue.[46] However, it soon developed that Collins and Rascoe could not agree on editorial policies—they disagreed mainly over the selections to be used—and Rascoe sent Collins his letter of resignation on April 13, 1928.[47]

Rascoe was equally busy during the years 1928 through 1930. In 1928 and 1929 (until the Crash), Rascoe actively and successfully played the stock market. In February, 1929, *A Bookman's Daybook*, edited by C. Hartley Grattan, was published. In March, 1929, the Rascoe family moved to 42 Stuyvesant Avenue, Larchmont, New York, from Mamaroneck, where it had been living since 1925. From February, 1929, until October, 1930, Rascoe wrote monthly book reviews for *Plain Talk;* and from August, 1929, until June, 1930, he was that magazine's associate editor. From February through December, 1930, he was an editorial adviser for McBride's Publishing Company. He visited Cabell in January, 1930, and spoke to the Richmond Writers Club while there. During these years he was also literary critic—and had been since 1924—writing monthly pieces for *Arts and Decoration* and *The Detroit Athletic Club News.* He was so busy editing and writing, he told Cabell on March 31, 1930, that he had had to take an apartment in town in order to get all of his work done.

VII *New Jobs and Two New Books*

Jobs weren't so plentiful for Rascoe in the early 1930's as they had been in the 1920's, but he nearly always managed to find something. For a few months in the early part of 1931 he contributed daily to the book page of the *New York American,* writing on books three times each week and on any subject of his choosing on the two alternate days. From October, 1931, until July, 1933, he was a literary critic for the *New York Sun*, writing another "Bookman's Day Book" column that he and Laurence Stallings alternated in doing.

In 1931 and 1932 he suffered from serious money problems—he no longer had any money in the bank, his expenses exceeded his income, and he was in poor health. After July 24, 1931, when his father died, he had to concern himself with several lawsuits to get his father's California estate settled; and he quarreled bitterly with his mother and two younger brothers over how the settlement was being handled. And Mary Fanton Roberts, editor of *Arts and Decoration*, wrote Rascoe on January 26, 1932, saying that, because of the "financial depression," the budget was being cut wherever possible; his column was, therefore, being temporarily suspended.

In this period Rascoe began a different kind of fight in his *Sun* articles. In March, April, and May, 1932, he wrote a number of articles attacking communism and communist sympathizers—and clearly set forth his own basic political, economic, and social ideas, which he fought for repeatedly in the 1930's, 1940's, and even in the 1950's. In Chicago he was a believer in socialism about the time of World War I, but he now criticized Marx's "economic pathology" in *Das Kapital* and wrote that it was a "flight from common sense" to believe that "under so-called capitalism people are made vile and ignoble and perverted."[48] In these remarkably farsighted articles Rascoe tried to lessen the appeal of communism to the younger intellectuals and writers by logical argument and by satire, predicting that they would be duped if they accepted its premises and believed its promises.

Somewhat earlier, on October 13, 1931, Earle H. Balch, of Putnam's, had written to Rascoe suggesting that he write *Titans of Literature: From Homer to the Present.* Rascoe agreed to write the book and received an advance of two thousand dollars from Putnam's. *Titans* was published on November 1, 1932, a few days after Rascoe's fortieth birthday. Lynn Carrick of Putnam's reported to Rascoe on April 12, 1933, that so far the total sales of *Titans* had been approximately ten thousand copies, and that this sale, considering the times, was "remarkably fine"; the book was "highly successful." Rascoe was given another two thousand-dollars advance to do a sequel, to be called *Prometheans.* On May

16, 1933, Rascoe wrote to Thomas H. Breeze, the San Francisco lawyer who had handled his interests in the settlement of his father's estate, about this new book, which he was already writing: "Prometheus, the fire-bringer, brought warmth and the implements and instincts for civilization to mortals and these are the qualities I hold to be virtues of my lesser Titans."

In December, 1932, Rascoe became literary critic of *Esquire*, writing a monthly column about books. He edited (with Groff Conklin) *The Smart Set Anthology* in 1934; Rascoe wrote the Introduction, a history of the magazine, for the *Anthology*. From 1934 until 1937 he was an editorial adviser for Doubleday, Doran and Company; and from 1927 until 1937 he was also on the editorial board of The Literary Guild of America (a subsidiary of Doubleday).

VIII   *A Personal Tragedy*

One disaster after another befell Rascoe in 1936 and 1937. In the fall of 1936, after their daughter Ruth Rascoe had entered Northwestern University, the Rascoes went to Vermont for a vacation. While they were there, their twenty-two-year-old son, Burton, Jr., who had remained at home in Larchmont, became despondent and took his own life on September 19. Crushed by their son's suicide, the Rascoes went to Chicago, remaining there five weeks before returning to the Hotel White in New York City to live; but in the spring of 1937 they sold their house in Larchmont and moved from the hotel into an apartment at 310 West 85th Street. In the January, 1937, issue of *Esquire* Rascoe wrote about his son's death as, he told Cabell, "a spontaneous temporary relief from suffering."[49] His relief was temporary; for on June 19, 1938, in filling out an application for a Guggenheim Foundation Fellowship for 1939, he gave as his permanent address Ferncliff Cemetery, Scarsdale, New York;[50] Rascoe's son was buried there.

In May, 1937, Rascoe's autobiography, *Before I Forget*, was published. For a rest after writing this book, Rascoe and his wife took a trip to Burlingame, California, to visit Rascoe's mother. They stopped in Chicago, where Rascoe spoke to the Chicago Women's Club in May, finally arriving in Burlingame on July 5. On July 21, Doubleday, Doran notified Rascoe that Max Annenberg was suing him and Doubleday for $250,000 for libelous material in *Before I Forget*. Rascoe's first reaction was to sit down that day and write Annenberg a letter appealing to Annenberg's better nature; Rascoe explained that he had tried to make his life "mean something in the way of an honest, even if faulty, account of things seen, heard and felt." But he thought better of this letter, and did not send it. On August 24, 1937, he gave a check for twenty-five hundred dollars to the DeWitt, Van Aken and Nast law firm to represent him. The suit dragged on for years—until November 1, 1939—before it was finally dropped when Annenberg agreed to forget the matter and Doubleday to delete the pages from remaining copies of the book. The cost in legal fees and investigators' fees to Rascoe had been eight thousand dollars.[51]

But the blows were to continue. In 1937, Rascoe was asked to formulate a prospectus for *Ken*, a new magazine which David Smart was planning to publish. Rascoe, who prepared the prospectus, refused to edit the magazine, explaining in a letter to Smart that "For nearly three years [Doubleday, Doran] had been working on me to take the full-time job of Editor on the retirement of Russell Doubleday; but I knew that to do so would mean the end of my writing career, so I told them frankly and often that I would not take the job at $50,000 a year."[52] He told Smart that he had resigned two editorships in May of that year—his jobs as editorial adviser to Doubleday, Doran and as editor-in-chief of the Literary Guild. Later, an argument with Smart ensued over how much he should be paid for his work on the *Ken* prospectus, and Rascoe became so angry that he also resigned—in April, 1938 —his job as literary critic of *Esquire*. The first issue of the short-lived *Ken* was published on May 31, 1938.

The April 25, 1938, issue of *Newsweek* announced that it had secured the "exclusive services of Burton Rascoe" as "commentator on current books and the literary scene" and that he would replace Sinclair Lewis.[53] Rascoe's first column in *Newsweek*, entitled "'Scholars' Mugg the Camera," was a defense of Lloyd Eschleman's *Moulders of Destiny*, which, Rascoe said, had been "slapped down in several reviews by the phiddle-de-dees, notably by Samuel Chew [of Bryn Mawr], and Crane Brinton" of Harvard. But, Rascoe continued, "The Chews and Brintons, the Donald A. Roberts and the Edith Hamiltons as book reviewers are like the hams of Hollywood who mugg the camera or the small vaudeville actors who are callously expert in stealing a bow."[54] Donald A. Roberts and Edith Hamilton had wounded Rascoe deeply when they had ridiculed, in the December 31, 1932, issue of *The Saturday Review of Literature*, his scholarships in *Titans of Literature*.[55] He was never able to forget their criticism or to forgive them. In this defense of Eschleman's book Rascoe also took a slap at the "Holy Roman Catholic Church . . . [which] now, shorn of temporal power, restricted in spiritual power, [is] trying to make a deal with Hitler."

In July, 1938, Rascoe taught a short course in professional writing at the University of Oklahoma, and he visited Shawnee and the surrounding area. That year he also edited *An American Reader* for Putnam's, writing the Introduction and introductory essays for the different sections of the anthology. To Rex Smith, his managing editor at *Newsweek*, Rascoe expressed in letters on August 30, 1938, and September 19, 1938, his strong anti-British feelings; he told Smith that he believed that there was collusion between Britain and Germany. Wherever he could in 1939, Rascoe enthusiastically helped to promote H. C. Peterson's *Propaganda for War, 1914–1917: The Campaign Against American Neutrality*, a book which proved (to Rascoe) that it was British propaganda that had caused the United States to get involved in World War I. On September 7, 1939, Smith notified Rascoe that he had cut Rascoe's column that week because of a lack of space, necessitated by the war. Rascoe felt that he was being censored, and on September 11, 1939, he resigned from *Newsweek*.

IX *Anti-Communistic–Anti-War Struggles*

Long before Rascoe resigned, however, he had found an outlet for what he had to say about political matters. Since March 14, 1939, he had been writing a New York column, "Burton Rascoe Says," for the Shawnee (Oklahoma) News Company, publishers of the *Shawnee Morning News* and *Shawnee Evening Star*. In these columns he wrote about many subjects, but mainly about his obsessive fear that Britain would get this country into another war, though he predicted on August 28, 1939, that there would be no war in Europe within three years. The last of these Shawnee columns, on September 19, 1939, was about the Hitler-Stalin pact of August 23.

This non-aggression treaty between Hitler and Stalin seemed to Rascoe to justify his many attacks on communism in the 1930's and his more recent attacks on fascism. He had argued repeatedly that communism and fascism were two sides of the same coin, and the Stalin-Hitler pact, he felt, proved it. More importantly, he believed that this revelation about communism would bring about an increased acceptance of his own views on the nature and function of art and literature. Addressing the annual luncheon of the Southern Women's National Democratic Organization in New York on January 27, 1940, he contended that literature is not "a social document intended to represent conditions and indict a whole people for permitting these conditions to exist." He maintained that for a correct theory of art and literature the critics must return to Aristotle's *Rhetoric* and *Poetics;* it was "irrelevant critical fallacies" that caused Ellen Glasgow's *The Romantic Comedians* to be labeled "escapist," "afflicted with bourgeois ideology," and "utterly without social significance." But things have changed already since the Hitler-Stalin pact, he reported; and they would get better: "crippled values will be restored to health and vigor...."[56]

Throughout most of 1940 Rascoe was literary critic for *The American Mercury,* and he devoted many of his columns to helping restore these older, healthy values. In a group review of Cabell's *Hamlet Had an Uncle,* Nathan's *Encyclopedia of the Theatre,* and Mencken's *Happy Days,* Rascoe attacked much of the literature of the 1930's because, he said, it was bad art and was poorly written. But Cabell, Nathan, and Mencken, "each in his individual way, has a rich and varied vocabulary, a sense of the high importance of syntax, and a proper appreciation of the tone, texture, color, appearance and meaning of words in expressing subtleties and shades of ideas in giving distinction, life and cogency to images. They are neither one-finger virtuosi nor mental hermits who have shut themselves in the dismal Marxian cave to listen only to the roar of hollow conks."[57] In his April review, he analyzed Erskine Caldwell's latest novel, *Trouble in July,* to show that it was Marxist propaganda;[58] in May, he reviewed Richard Wright's *Native Son,* finding its explicit "message" "utterly loathsome and utterly unsupportable."[59] In December, in his last column to appear in *The American Mercury,* he reviewed new books by Hemingway, Thomas Wolfe, and James T. Farrell.

Hemingway's political confusion and naïveté in *For Whom the Bell Tolls* proved, Rascoe said, that Hemingway was "the most infantile-minded writer of great talent in our time"; Wolfe's *You Can't Go Home Again* showed that he had achieved maturity before he died; and Farrell achieved maturity at about the age of thirty, after the second volume of the *Studs Lonigan* trilogy.[60]

In 1940 Rascoe again waged his own war—in articles, books, and letters—to keep the United States out of the war in Europe. On August 1 he wrote to the Authors' League of America to protest the League's Bulletin being used to advocate American intervention in the war on Britain's behalf. In a heated exchange of letters with Van Wyck Brooks over Archibald MacLeisch's *The Irresponsibles,* Rascoe told Brooks that he believed that "Basically, [MacLeish's] balleyhoo for his new electric-belt vigoro philosophy is merely a specious argument that we should become nazi-totalitarian and go to war at once on the side of a completely Hitlerized British government."[61]

Then the same thing happened that had happened at *Newsweek*: a column of Rascoe's was rejected. On November 29, Eugene Lyons, editor of *The American Mercury*, wrote to tell Rascoe that he was rejecting "Ladies Who Want Hell" because it was a political attack on Clare Boothe, Edna St. Vincent Millay, and Dorothy Thompson. Later, in an undated letter to Quincy Howe, Rascoe explained that "I resigned from the American Mercury when Gene Lyons declined to print a piece of mine entitled 'Ladies Who Want Hell,' attacking Edna Millay's new war-mongering jingles, Clare Boothe and Dotty Thompson...." In another letter on December 19, Rascoe angrily denounced Lyons because Lyons had attacked the non-interventionist magazine, *Uncensored,* of which Rascoe was a sponsor.[62]

X *Fails To Find Publishers*

Rascoe had no success at all with his books in 1940. On May 3, Curtice Hitchcock notified Rascoe that Reynal and Hitchcock had turned down his novel, *The Boomer*. Lloyd Eschleman wrote to the Frederick A. Stokes Publishing Company on June 3 and said that he was not going to finish editing *Rascoe's Roundup* (more of Rascoe's "Day Book" material) for Stokes. And, on October 30, George Shively of the Stokes company wrote to Rascoe's agent,

William Lengel, that Rascoe's book, *Lest We Forget*, a book about how Britain dragged America into World War I, was not acceptable to Stokes.

In 1940–41 Rascoe gave editorial advice to Oskar Piest, a New York bookseller and publisher. In January 8, 1941, Fulton Oursler, editor-in-chief of *Liberty Magazine*, notified Rascoe that "... your short short story, INITIATION, published in the April 13, 1940, issue of *Liberty*, has won seventh bonus of $100.00."[63] He had been paid two hundred dollars for the story in 1940. From August 25 until September 8, 1941, Rascoe reviewed books for the *New York World Telegram*, replacing Harry Hansen who was on vacation. He also wrote one book in 1941, *Belle Starr: "The Bandit Queen,"* for Random House; and, in November, he sold an article on Western outlaws to *True Magazine*.

Thus, 1942 began bleakly for Rascoe. His financial situation had grown desperate. To Cabell, he wrote on February 5 that he had "a job writing a literary column three times a week" for the new *Chicago Sun*. "But," he said, "I am broke. Hazel and I are living in two furnished rooms, with bath and kitchenette, and Hazel is doing all the cooking; our goods are in storage; two books of mine went dead on me by the outbreak of the war—two books finished in manuscript—because they were books no publisher would take...." His *Sun* column was dropped on June 1, and he wrote on June 23 to Louis Paul: "Desperately been looking for a job. So far none. Have sold some magazine stuff. But hardly enough to keep us going...." In August he took a job writing copy for the advertising agency of Batten, Barton, Durstine and Osborn; but in December he was let go. Shortly before this, however, he had been hired as drama critic, replacing John Mason Brown, by the *New York World-Telegram*.

Rascoe wrote dramatic criticism for the *World-Telegram* from October 20, 1942, until April 4, 1946. He then quit, he told Cabell, after the executive editor had declined to print his hard, "roasting" review of the Old Vic Company's performance of *Henry IV, Part I*. This piece was the third held out on him at the *World-Telegram*, he said; and he "was getting pretty fed up with the chore anyhow." He told Cabell that in 1944 he had also "sat in as chief editorial writer (in addition to writing at least three theatre pieces a week) for 10 weeks while the chief editorial writer was on sick leave, had sat in twice for Harry Hansen as book-reviewer, while he was on vacation," and had written his monthly article for the *Detroit Athletic Club News*.[64]

On June 13, 1946, Rascoe was again notified by Doubleday, Doran that he and Doubleday were being sued, this time by Labron Burton for libelous material in *Before I Forget;* but this suit was settled out of court for three thousand dollars. The second volume of Rascoe's autobiography, *We Were Interrupted,* about Rascoe's work in the 1920's, was published in 1947. That year and the next Rascoe reviewed American literature and the book publishing business in the *American Annual,* and he contributed "Tendencies in the U.S. Drama" (from 1937 through 1946) to *10 Eventful Years,* published by the *Encyclopedia Britannica.* He told Cabell on October 11, 1947, that he was writing for *Plain Talk* for one hundred dollars a month "and wherever else I could pick up a penny, while biding my time." He was also asked to review Cabell's forty-fifth book, *Let Me Lie,* in the *New York Herald Tribune* that year.

From October, 1948, until April, 1949, Rascoe was director of the Adelphi Center of Creative Arts (Playwrights Educational Theatre) at Adelphi College in Garden City, New York. He produced, directed, and reviewed works by amateur playwrights; but, after arguing violently with some of the players and with the president of Adelphi College over the policy of financing the theater—Rascoe wanted to make it self-supporting—he soon quit. He was also appointed in the spring semester of 1949 to teach a course in playwriting at Adelphi College at a salary of five hundred dollars.[65]

From 1950 to 1953, Rascoe found only a very limited interest in his work; he was almost forgotten. From the Avon Publishing Company he did get some hack work: in December, 1949, he wrote an Introduction for Calder Willingham's *End as a Man* for two hundred dollars; he did editorial revisions on James Aswell's *The Midsummer Fires* for one hundred dollars; in 1950, he wrote an Introduction for Calder Willingham's *Geraldine Bradshaw;* and, in 1952, he wrote an Introduction for James G. Huneker's *Painted Veils* for one hundred and fifty dollars. And, in 1953, he did some editorial work for Gold Medal Books.

To Cabell, he wrote on December 22, 1952: "It can't be news to you that I am not in rapport with the literary minds of New York's best circles and have not been for some years and so I have

had to make a living by writing in an almost furtive manner."
He described the kind of work he had been doing: "I have been
writing (or finding an outlet for things I have wanted to say) in
The Freeman and Human Events, which are published rather
clandestinely; and I have been able to make a very precarious
living by reading manuscripts, writing for magazines like True,
Today's Woman, Real Detective Stories and compiling an anthology." On June 1, 1953, Rascoe informed Cabell that "I am
writing a weekly book review for a syndicate and I ordinarily
write from one to three unsigned editorials for Human Events in
Washington, [and I] sell an occasional article...." He was writing a weekly book review for Classic Features Syndicate. In July,
the Rascoes visited—for the last time—the Cabells in Ophelia,
Virginia.

XI   *Final Newspaper Column—Death*

Beginning April 20, 1954, Rascoe started reviewing television
shows for Classic Features Syndicate, a job he held for the next
three years. He wrote Cabell on September 28, 1956, that he had
a teletype machine in his apartment, where, after watching television play rehearsals at the studios, he filed a "daily stint of 650
words of the 'TV First-Nighter' column to the five Newhouse
papers in the vicinity of New York and the Harrisburg paper that
print my stuff." In these "TV-First-Nighter" columns Rascoe was
personal, colloquial, argumentative, and often controversial. He
filed his last column on Monday, March 18, 1957; and the next
day he died in his apartment at 525 East 89th Street, New York
City.

CHAPTER 2

Critical Theories and Practice

WRITING IN 1947 about his literary criticism in the 1920's, Rascoe stated that "... I had no fixed critical program, no intractable theory from which to proceed in a straight line, trying to make life and literature conform to that theory. I hadn't any such fixed idea and I haven't now." He believed rather that "A fixed idea or an arbitrary theory in criticism demands a consistency that is foolish in an evolving world; it cuts one off from an infinite number of sources of pleasure." And, furthermore, he continued, "... the critic is likely, very shortly, to adopt an entirely contrary set of convictions." He showed how Irving Babbitt, Paul Elmer More, Van Wyck Brooks, Edmund Wilson, and Stuart Pratt Sherman had had fixed ideas or critical theories that had forced them to ridiculous conclusions or how they had had to replace their worn-out or untenable theories with new ones or even their opposites.[1]

And in his Journal (BRC), Rascoe also wrote that "I have no theories. I have only impressions and sensations"; "Sherman says to criticize one must have a program. This is precisely what is fatal to intelligent criticism. Babbitt has a program and his program carefully held before his eyes always blinds him to what is before him on the printed page." Rascoe was even more anti-theoretical in "Reflections on Aim and Intention," his preface to *Before I Forget*, describing his autobiography as a history "of an almost frantic avoidance of philosophy, out of an experience and belief that one can have a philosophy about an action only when it is too late to be of any good [and] that life is an adventure so unpredictable that to espouse an intransigent system of thought and belief is either to confuse one's life with unsupportable conflicts and contradictions or so to delude oneself as to give the appearance of hypocrisy."[2] From these and many other, similar statements we can see that Rascoe accepted no definite theory or philosophy of criticism; that he believed only that the value and quality of any criticism depends entirely on the critic's taste, personality, temperament, individuality, and experience.

Actually, however,—and this at first may seem paradoxical—so large a part of his criticism dealt with problems of esthetics that Harry Hansen once wrote to him that "I think of you as strongly influenced by European backgrounds, especially the French, writing a fluid, finished style, rich in allusions to non-American and non-midwestern backgrounds, interested in questions of aesthetics, technique, style, etc., that frequently originate abroad."[3] The truth is that Rascoe did have theoretical standards—although he frequently *said* that he had no program of esthetics and often attacked those who did have such programs; and—although he often contradicted himself, changed his mind, or said that he could not make up his mind on certain esthetic or philosophical questions—all of his work hangs together on several major threads.

I *Imaginative and Emotional Truth*

The central thread of Rascoe's esthetics was his Romantic belief that reality exists only in the imagination. He felt that the artist should not even try to create an "imitation of nature," a verisimilitude, a surface or photographic reality; indeed, it would be impossible to do so. Rascoe explained, in a letter to Edward Bjorkman in 1954, that he had always been a champion of Realism and an opponent of Pollyannaism, but that "... realism in fiction or the drama is not reality; it is a presentation of a set of imagined characters in an imagined situation and involved in a problem requiring a solution that is acceptable as good sense universally, because the imagined characters and the imagined situations are credible and because the solution is an acceptable moral attitude or cogent point of view."[4]

Art, then, only symbolizes reality, which can only be symbolized, never experienced directly; but this symbolization is an absolute necessity: to the artist, who needs to create these symbols; and to the person, who needs to experience them. Writing about such imaginative exercises in *Titans*, Rascoe said that D. H. Lawrence came "closer perhaps than any other novelist to the nerve edge of our inner experience. No realist has ever written a realistic novel; to do so is impossible. Lawrence comes closest to those realities which are really incommunicable."[5] Art, therefore, must symbolize the truth and "reality" of the artist's own inner experience; it must be, in other words, a "vision" of life, either emotional or intellectual truth transmuted by the artist's individual sense of order into symbolic expression.

This was another of Rascoe's major premises: that the artist has a special vision. Using Joseph Conrad's statement of his aim as a novelist, Rascoe once explained what the novelist meant:

> "My task," writes Joseph Conrad in the preface to "The Nigger of the Narcissus," is, by the power of the written word, to make you hear, to make you feel—it is, before all, to make you see. That and no more, and it is everything. If I succeed, you shall find there according to your deserts: encouragement, consolation, fear, charm—all you demand, and perhaps also that glimpse of truth for which you had forgotten to ask."
>
> That, in epitome, is the creed of a novelist, who by common critical consent, has beyond all others of his time approached by way of the novel the plasticity of sculpture, the color of painting, and the suggestiveness of music, to which he in common with all serious artists in fiction aspires.
>
> You will note that he says nothing whatever about "moral purpose," "vital problems," "slices of life," "bringing out the best in man," "showing the triumph of good over evil," or "the triumph of evil over good," or any of the nonsensical and irrelevant catch phrases of the fifth-rate fictioneer. He is intent upon conveying to you his vision of life as an artist and nothing else. His media are words and nothing else.[6]

The artist, Rascoe continued in this explanation, only symbolizes truth or "reality" as he sees it: "If you find him reverent or irreverent, optimistic or pessimistic, mellowed or cynical, clean or offensive, helpful or harmful, that is your interpretation of him and something with which he has, as an artist, no concern. He has as an aim not one of these antitheses, and if by chance he achieves one it is without intent, even, perhaps, without his knowledge."

Indeed, the true artist in only expressing his view of reality even though he is ostensibly saying something else, as was George Bernard Shaw, for instance, in *Saint Joan*: ". . . the elaborate argument of Shaw about the treatment of Joan of Arc by her contemporaries is related to Joan only by spiritual marriage. Shaw is talking about Shaw and his contemporaries even when he is using the symbols Joan, the Inquisitor, the Dauphin, Warwick and the

Bishop of Beauvais. He is talking about Shaw when he brings up the trial of Socrates and likens the trial of Joan to it. He is talking about Shaw when he asks, in the last speech of his play, when will people recognize their saints when they appear among them."[7]

Consequently, to Rascoe, even the writing of history became an esthetic rather than a "scientific" problem. He believed that "history must depend on insufficient and inadequate testimony; that the stuff from which [historians] weave their fabrics, the accounts and documents of the time, must be at least as unreliable as the testimony given in a criminal court." And so, he argued, historical "reality" could only be perceived imaginatively:

> History is a reflection of known, reported and recorded events cast through a temperament. There can be no science of history because science is an accumulation of known and tested data, out of which new hypotheses may arise and which may be turned into practical use, whereas history has to do with events; and our knowledge of events is, finally, uncertain because it is subject to the vagaries of human credulity. Those who attempt to write history, in fact, are condemned (no matter how factually and dully they write) to approach the task as an aesthetic problem to be solved rather than as a scientific or even a logical one; for they must give unity of concept to a literary design.

Therefore, because the record of historical facts is necessarily unreliable, the historian and the novelist are essentially alike in their tasks:

> So I would ask that historians accept the consequence that their craft is fundamentally aesthetic, rather than scientific—that in trying to give unity to the heterogeneous data they have about events, personalities, and periods, they are dealing not so much in scientific hypothesis as in the creation of literary design.
>
> If precedent is asked for this, we have it in the world's ability to characterize most of the truly great in history by a word or phrase. Herodotus was curious; Thuycydides was judicious; Livy was a compiler; Caesar's histories are a military commander's official reports; Tacitus wrote primarily to entertain; Suetonius was a sensationalist; Plutarch was a hero-worshipper (as was Carlyle later); Voltaire was a socio-political irritant; Montesquieu was a rationalistic investigator; Michelet was a poetic generalizer; Gibbon was an erudite embodiment of eighteenth century unbanity; Macaulay was a bourgeois Whig litterateur with an unfatigu-

ing style. These characterizations do not tell the whole story about any one of these historians; but the point is that it is impossible to describe any one of them without pronouncing an aesthetic judgment.

This not only would make history immensely more entertaining, but would preserve to the general knowledge, the fruit of much painstaking research that now gathers dust in the archives, because it is simply unreadable.[8]

Like the novelist, the historian must take a point of view; therefore he is, like any artist, selective in his presentation.

Rascoe's own histories of ideas and biographical studies, *Titans* and *Prometheans,* and his autobiographies, *Before I Forget* and *We Were Interrupted,* assume this Romantic view of history; and they illustrate Rascoe's views about the writing of history, though his intentions were misunderstood by many of the reviewers of these books. In an undated typescript (BRC), probably written shortly after *Prometheans* was published, Rascoe described his method of writing *Titans* and *Prometheans*:

"Titans of Literature" and "Prometheans" were written entirely out of my memory. I had no notes; I did not use standard works of reference, no encyclopedias or histories of literature. My memory told me accurately on what page any quotation or reference I wanted could be found and, instead of relying upon my memory to quote accurately, I would make a notation in my manuscript telling my secretary to type out the quotation on such and such a page. I thought it was much better to do this. It had never been done before. My book should be, I thought, a distillation of all I had got from history and from other literature, a residium of my reading, observation and experience. They were not to be compilations. If errors of memory should creep in, I thought they should remain in, lest corrections invalidate the testimony of the book. And besides, dates were, I considered, unimportant to my book except in a vague way; certainly I was not writing the sort of book people would be looking into to establish or verify dates: there are thousands of books for these purposes.

Yet some of the reviews denounced me and the book wholly on the score of having given the date of Goethe's death inaccurately. Most of the other dates were, happily, accurate, but not because of any special care of mine—largely by the accident of memory,—yet this inaccurate date I gave for Goethe's death formed the fulcrum on which a pedagog from Columbia University used the lever of a whole column of abuse to raise me to the high level of William Lyon Phelps' disapproval.

Shortly after *Prometheans* was published, late in 1933, Rascoe wrote to Cabell discussing the book: "I know that the [essays on] St. Mark, Petronius, Lucian and Apuleius are good; that the Nietzsche and Lawrence are good as far as they go; that the Dreiser is fair; the Cabell slipshod, and the Aretino lousy. But what is good is very, very good, containing some fine examples of oblique writing. I am not particularly surprised that no reviewer so far has shown any signs of seeing what I was writing in that long first chapter."[9] Later, in a letter to Dreiser, he explained what he had meant by "oblique" writing. He told Dreiser that 'Prometheans' is more subjective [than *Titans*] and it has more directly to do with what is going on today. I think of it [being] as much about Communism, Fascism, and the Catholic Church as about the figures I write about."[10] Much later, in a letter to Milo Sutliff, who was then editor of the Family Reading Club, Rascoe was more specific; he explained why *Prometheans* would not be a good selection for a family book club:

> The first chapter of "Prometheans," on St. Mark (ostensibly, although it actually is about something else and is a very profound essay in philosophic irony) would be disturbing to any of the orthodox beliefs—Catholic, Protestant, Judaic or Communistic (the point of that essay is that the Marxian concept is a religion very like that of the Essene sect of Judaism which became known as Christianity and that just as the powerful and aggressive saw in this concept a source of tremendous demagogic power and so founded the Church, under Charlemagne, wherein Church and State were united in dictatorial power, so also Stalin and his group found the religion of Communism an instrument of tremendous power that actually denies, in reality, all the Marxian tenets, just as the Holy Roman Catholic Church was an aggrandizement which was a denial of the principles of the Essene or Christian religion).[11]

Rascoe learned much later that Victor Gollancz, an English publisher, had refused to publish *Titans* because "It is an American book in the worst sense. . . ." This remark infuriated Rascoe; and, defending his *Titans*, he wrote in a letter to Gollancz that "culture for the masses, not only for the few . . . underlay the whole conception of my 'Titans of Literature,'" and that "I was trying to bring to the minds of sensitive and appreciative natural men and women the things of the mind and spirit and the heritage of literature as well as I could, as a living experience, not as dead lumber or exercises to be learned by rote and forgotten or to furnish tag lines of 'culture' or 'sensational' successes like you, who have a sense of merchandising."[12]

Rascoe himself preferred works like Georg Brandes' *The Main Currents in Nineteenth Century Literature*, which was an "unfailingly satisfying" literary history because it was "a work of creative imagination."[13] And, in the notes (BRC) he made for a lecture to the Chicago Women's Club, delivered in May, 1937, he named several histories that he thought were greater creative works than some fiction: "Gibbon's 'Decline and Fall of the Roman Empire' is surely a greater work of creative art than, say, Rebecca West's 'The Thinking Reed'"; and "'The Memoirs of Saint-Simeon' are not merely records of events—they are the phenomena of life seen through a temperament. Lytton Strachey is more creative, say, than some one who follows the formula of boy-meets-girl . . . of successful magazine fiction."

Rascoe often stated his belief "that the psychology of fictionists like Dostoievsky, Hardy, Chekhov, Maupassant and Conrad is more generally reliable than the psychology of historians and biographers who perform under the aegis of truth and fact a work of imaginative construction just as liable to error and misrepresentation as the effort of a defective fictionist whose characters do not follow a logical or inevitable series of characteristic acts."[14] Even so, the novelist is not a psychologist, Rascoe thought; and his work should not be a psychological treatise:

> . . . the primary aim of the novelist is to make you feel—to make you comprehend not through the intellect but through the emotions. Explanations are a sorry substitute for the imagination: they do very well in an explanatory thesis. Character in a novel is best, most artistically, most inescapably established through action; the other sort of thing is critical analysis. . . . What the Freudians have done for literature is to familiarize many laymen with some of the more obvious motives that lie back of human actions, and thus make them more understanding and sympathetic readers of works of great imagination and verisimilitude, less easily taken in by sentimentality, less patient with the palpably unreal. It has supplied critics, too, with new analytical material.[15]

A formal knowledge of the actual rules of human psychology was not important to the artist, Rascoe continued: "Dostoievsky is probably the greatest psychological novelist that ever lived, but he was that because he had what amounts to profound intuitions regarding the heart and mind of mankind. If one had asked him to explain why one of his characters acted thus and so, he probably would have replied, 'I don't know. He just did. That's the way I saw him.'"

A corollary to this central belief of Rascoe's in the "reality" of imaginative truth was his belief that the feelings or emotions were more "real" than the intellect. Like Hawthorne's, his was a "truth of the human heart." He commented in his "Day Book" on Hugh Elliot's *Human Character*, saying that he had found verification for this belief:

> The most revolutionary conclusion of [the most advanced modern] psychologists is, perhaps, that both intellect and will are feeble faculties subordinate to, and dependent upon, emotion, and that in the last analysis emotion is the most important factor in human character. Whereas the earlier psychologists divided the mind into intellect, feeling and will and concentrated their attention upon the intellect (because it was the easiest to study and because it was the attribute which separated men from the brutes), the modern psychologists are forced to the rather obvious conclusion that thought itself is only an emotion.[16]

This truth artists understood best, Rascoe thought; but scientists were beginning to understand it.

This belief that the emotions are manifestations of the essential self, which art symbolizes, was the basis of the Introduction Rascoe wrote in 1937 for Oscar Wilde's *The Ballad of Reading Gaol.* According to Rascoe, Wilde's mistake was that he reversed the roles played by the intellect and the emotions in the creation of art; and, consequently, his art suffered:

> The ordinary, the humane sentiments and emotions are the very stuff of the greatest literature. Because Oscar Wilde stifled them in himself and chose always to exist and to attitudinize on the plane of the artificial, he never rose above being a brilliant second-rate writer and he degenerated rapidly into an inferior man.
>
> He had at his command the words of humility and pride and respect and sorrow and bitterness and he used them, but they were hollow words carrying no warmth or feeling of conviction. His genius was for wit and comedy, of the play of mind upon

events and feelings, of commentary that is sharp and stinging, urbane and amusing, of the intellect and not of the heart.

Only rarely did he key his expression to sad, tender, or tragic themes; and when he did he commonly failed. . . . Thus it was that in nearly all the verse that Oscar Wilde wrote which has to do with sentiment there is the failure of the man who could think but who could not feel. Even in "The Ballad of Reading Gaol," where the haunting melody and the funereal beat are flawlessly sustained to give one the feeling of imminent death and of the effect that thoughts of death has upon others condemned in prison, the most memorable line, "Each man kills the thing he loves," is a commentary, a generalization, which is not even specifically allied to the story or derived from it but super-imposed upon it as a moral tag-line or philosophical observation.[17]

Writing about Wilde again in 1949, Rascoe said that "All of [Wilde's] writings are primarily the products of the intellect rather than of feeling; they are mechanically contrived by a superb mechanician, to be sure, but a mechanic nevertheless; there is a hint of artificiality about the *expression* of his most deeply felt emotions. And it is the trade of the actor to counterfeit emotion, to produce the semblance of actuality by artificial means, without feeling any emotions whatever."[18]

II *The Autonomous Life of Art*

A second major thread running through Rascoe's esthetics was his belief that art has an autonomous life or existence, and that this existence is meant to symbolize an emotional experience, not to express an ethical viewpoint. Though the artist is always free to choose his subject, he must present it artistically—that is, he must never *use* his art for intellectual or social purposes. This means that the novelist, for example, must never intrude into his novel to make his own comments. Dreiser frequently made this mistake, and Rascoe criticized him for it; in an article on *The Hand of the Potter* Rascoe wrote that the first three acts of the play were excellent but were nullified by a "nonsensical irrelevant sermon as a fourth." He likened the first three acts to the "peddler's deft and ingenious prelude to attract the crowd," after which "when interest is assured out will come the pink pills for human ills." That is, in the fourth act in the mouth of a reporter commenting upon the "story," Dreiser "puts a long disquisition voicing his own opinions on the case at hand, his vague and facile philosophy of chemical compounds, and his curious jumble of current theories of perverts in general." And that, Rascoe concluded, was frequently Dreiser's fault as an artist: "he usurps the function of Deity, and he is so tiresomely and uninterestingly moral. . . . He cannot resist the temptation to preach, to advise, to comment." This tendency, Rascoe believed, caused Dreiser to "botch," "deface," or "weaken" much of his fiction.[19]

On this fundamental critical principle—that didacticism of any sort was disastrous to work of art—Rascoe based his review in 1918 of *Some Modern Novelists*, by Helen Thomas Follett and Wilson Follett: ". . . the didactic novel is as ephemeral, per se, as a book review. It can hope for permanency only so far as its style, distinction, and constructive symmetry completely hide the fact that it was written for a purpose." The Folletts did not understand this principle of art, and in their book they had assumed "that literature is, at its best, an elaborate decalogue, telling us what we should and should not do; they would, by personal preference, have it preach democracy and human brotherhood." In this same review Rascoe gave examples to support his thesis, pointing out that John Galsworthy, "by becoming an ardent reformer, is becoming a less tolerable artist"; and H. G. Wells, "with his journalistic insight, anticipating the topics uppermost in men's minds for the moment and building novels about them, has cast his lot with the editorial writer.[20]

And, in a review of Henry B. Fuller's *On the Stairs*, Rascoe pointed out that many of the novelists who called themselves "Realists" were actually writing only short-lived arguments. He then reiterated his belief: "That which will survive will, unquestionably, be that which is most excellently written, and which has least to do with social problems." The reason for making this distinction, Rascoe explained, was that

. . . the real artist at novel writing is primarily distinguished by his apathies. He does not intrude his personal ethics upon his readers; he has no cult to propagate. He is alert, observant, analytic, keen to catch the recurrent trait of character. His experiences he refines, orders, subjects to infinite scrutiny and finally expresses in words that are apt, arbitrary in their usage, and woven together in such a manner as to give delight within themselves. He sees men as personalities rather than as types and he is interested in motives rather than in facile rules of conduct. He organizes his novel into a harmonious whole, giving it something of the aesthetic consequence of a well built symphony.[21]

Sherwood Anderson's *Winesburg, Ohio,* almost perfectly exemplified Rascoe's artistic ideal because "His personal ethics or beliefs obtrude, I think, but once, and that in the one unconvincing and manufactured story in the book—the story of the preacher who at night peeped through the window of his study into the bedroom of the pretty school teacher and afterwards delivered impassioned sermons on human frailty and temptation."[22] But not so with Ben Hecht's *Gargoyles:*

> The artistic fault with "Gargoyles" lies in the fact that too often Mr. Hecht resorts to editorial comment in character delineation instead of revealing character through action and dialogue. For that reason it is almost as much of a psychological essay as it is a work of fiction. Perhaps Mr. Hecht intended that it should be a combination of the two but the trouble with mixing them is that the figures do not emerge close enough to the reader to be tangible and palpably human and alive. In fine, Mr. Hecht tells us all about them—all their weaknesses, their hypocrisies, their meanness, their slimy sensuality, their vanities, their cheap romanticism, their platitudes, their lies, their contemptibleness, but he never introduces us to them.[23]

Rascoe based his review of Upton Sinclair's *Money Writes!* upon the critical assumption that art should not be used for propaganda purposes. He pictured Sinclair as a writer "always perched atop a soapbox, spreading his message abroad with a fine carelessness concerning facts and with generalizations that are compact with all the clichés of Socialist rhetoric." This book proved, Rascoe said, that Sinclair "simply does not know what art is all about. Your true artist is above time, place and circumstance; and it matters not a whit to him whether the country in which he finds himself is a monarchy or a democracy, or whether he is ruled by a kaiser, mikado, or the Republican party. Your true artist, in music, paint, sculpture or words, is passionately concerned with but one thing,—design; and a phrase, a surface, a combination of moves, or an alignment of colors is the only achievement or acquisition that gives him genuine pleasure." Furthermore, Sinclair's book was, Rascoe said, "the logical conclusion, the *reductio ad absurdum* to the arguments advanced in the writings of Van

Wyck Brooks, Lewis Mumford, Waldo Frank and all those critics who ring in polity to the confusion of aesthetics."[24]

In a typescript entitled "Literature Marches On!" Rascoe explained his belief that imaginative literature is organic, and that, although each age must produce its own literature, it cannot "be produced by fiat":

> Time, circumstances, conditions determine a literature; and, as a corollary, no time, circumstance or condition (however adverse it may seem) is ever impropitious; nor is genius ever lacking however slow we may be to recognize it.
>
> It is a too common misapprehension that a literature and, moreover a special kind of literature, may be produced by *fiat*. Thus in our very diffident and self-conscious past we had the frequent cry, "Let there be the Great American Novel!" And, in the minuscular Neo-Humanist *putsch* there was the cry, "Let there be New Humanist novels, poems and drama!"
>
> Still more recently there was the cry, "Let there be proletarian novels!"
>
> There are always some responses to such requests. The apt pupil always tries to do what teacher directs.... But they will not be expressions of what the writers "felt." They will not be articulations of some deep inner experience. They will not be ideas that flow from within, but ideas which were formulated in a pattern to conform with what the pupil thinks the teacher might like. They will not bring to the reader a feeling that this is something he has always vaguely apprehended but never was quite able to put into words.[25]

A critic that Rascoe admired was Sir Edmund Gosse, for Gosse had been able to live "through Victorianism and its reaction, the Yellow Nineties and the Shaw-Wells iconoclasm, the war and the disillusion after war, the neo-Thomist movement, the neo-Catholic revival, the reaction against the materialists of the nineteenth century and the potential anarchy of the theory of relatively, and among all these sweeping winds of doctrine [to keep] his interest and his enthusiasm centered upon pure literature." "Pure literature" Rascoe defined as being "a reflection of experience in life and not a propagandum or a panacea."[26]

III *The Critic as Artist*

A third major thread running through Rascoe's esthetics was his belief that criticism in itself is a separate art form; it is (or it should be) the creative expression of the critic's personality. Like Anatole France, Rascoe believed that criticism "was a record of the soul in the presence of masterpieces." He believed, as we have noted, that it was impossible to write objective criticism; although philosophically "An object may have an existence in itself," he said, "we can know that object only as its exists in our minds."[27] And he wrote in his journal (BRC) that "The critic's function is to re-create succinctly and in the terms of his own experience the artist's vision of the universe." Thus subjective criticism, he wrote, is "just as creative as novel writing" and is a "serious creative act."[28]

A great deal of Rascoe's writing was, therefore, about subjective criticism. For example, in a report in his "Day Book" of a conversation he had had with the music critic Charles Buchanan, Dr. Henry K. Marks, author of *Peter Middleton*, and Harrison Smith, of Harcourt, Brace and Company, Rascoe described and evaluated modern art and criticism as having

> ... definite characteristics which may be described as bad mannered, exhibitionistic, undisciplined, and even, from a certain point of view, vulgar; but that they also have the characteristics of vigor, warmth, curiosity, frankness and enthusiasm, which are the concomitants of the other qualities. This art and this criticism are natural products of the socio-economic conditions, plus our cultural inheritance and our reaction to it, and the tendency in art toward the "continual slight novelty." To protest against them is not only futile, but, as I see it, to protest against life itself. With this Mr. Buchanan violently disagrees.[29] He says the age is cursed by cleverness and superficiality and a flouting of standards; he believes in absolute standards of culture (which I think are a myth, and stultifying myths at that); and he told me he loathed and abominated and couldn't sit through a certain symphony ... but that he would not say so because many great appreciators of music had agreed that it is a masterpiece, and he would not flout his idiosyncracy in the face of that opinion. This is, I think, to take one's self far too seriously, and as Mr. Smith pointed out, it is to aid in imposing upon succeeding generations as inviolable and sacrosanct something which is merely a product of human skill and imagination. It is the way we have of so embalming classics in the oils of unction that one is never tempted to find out what they are really like.[30]

Each age must, therefore, create (or re-create) its own values in art, Rascoe argued. He did not, however, argue that subjective criticism was more infallible than any other kind of criticism; but, like history that was literature, it was more readable:

> Hazlitt was, I think, the greatest critic of his century because he was the most personal (every life of Hazlitt is made up almost entirely of quotations from his work), and certainly he was as fallible as any. No more fallible than Lemaître or Sainte-Beuve (who misjudged every one of importance of his own time) and other critics who are afflicted with the Jehovah complex and seek to be objective and remain unread. Who actually reads Sainte-Beuve nowadays? Mr. Buchanan knows and enjoys music. He is, or was, a critic. If he should say emphatically that he does not like that symphony the heavens would not fall, and perhaps he would give joy and reassurance to hundreds of other music lovers who loathe the symphony as much as he does, but endure it in pained silence and clap their hands and declare it is wonderful—because it is a classic.

In this same "Day Book" column Rascoe rebuked Kenneth Burke for turning away from the subjective "romantic moderns" to "didacticism and regimentation":

> Burke and Edmund Wilson, Jr., have stood out in my mind among all the younger critics as being the best informed, the most sensitive and most interesting. Something curious has happened to Burke. He, who in his efforts at story writing has been most bizarre and expressionistic and even downright incoherent, amazed me to-day by a vague discourse on the function of criticism, wherein he had the highest praise for Paul Elmer More, Irving Babbitt, and Matthew Arnold. He had definitely turned against "modernism" in arts and letters, and seems to have swung around entirely to didacticism and regimentation. He inclines to the More-Babbitt theory that Rousseau is the root of all romantic evil. "We must get away," he said, "from that individualism by which a sick man imposes upon the world his vicarious fulfillment of desires. Literature is now at a point where blind men write about the beauties of things they cannot see, and the halt and the lame write of the glories and exultation of walking. Such writing must inevitably be untrue to life, and seem silly to the sound and healthy. Rémy de Gourmont and Nietzsche were sick men whose writings were but compensations for what they missed in life. We must recognize that literature and the other arts, to be the best, must be true to the life and aspirations of the healthy majority of a race. If 'Ulysses' were read entirely as a joke, as one should

read Rabelais, and for the fun of the joke, it would not have a pernicious influence. But by most people it seemed to be taken seriously, as an accurate representation of life. It is as false on one side as Pollyanna is on the other." I quote all this as being intrinsically interesting and significant—significant in that it represents, as I see it, Burke's own reaction after a modernist debauch. I thought I could see, in a riotous, expressionistic, and ugly story he had in the "Little Review," the seed of a reaction which would flower into a defense of the sterile didacticism of Paul Elmer More.[31]

Rascoe then concluded that Burke, like other extreme Romantic moderns of every age, had merely revolted against something which he was fed up with; and he advised the Romantics to go moderately because decadence inevitably produces a formal and didactic literature, which he said he hoped had not already begun.

In the Preface of an unfinished book on American literature, Rascoe also rebuked the more objective critics for their caution and lack of enthusiasm; in this long work Rascoe argued that a lot of criticism was nonsense because of the critic's "incessant vagueness about what he considers meritorious in a literary work." As an example, he despaired, he said, of Van Wyck Brooks's reservations. Brooks "seems to be very often a man who is consciously writing for posterity and in holy terror of making a blunder to which some one, long after he is dead, will call attention. I never have read any writer who gave me a deeper impression of wanting to be right. Caution is a shining virtue; but it should not become an obsession."

Instead, Rascoe placed enthusiasm as an essential of criticism; for, he said, "It is only by enthusiasm that a critic may arouse interest in the work of an author." Most critics are not enthusiastic, "robust, liberal, and tolerant," however; they "are chinche and narrow and guarded in praise and vicious in rebuke. The trouble is that we are haunted by an ideal of perfection. This colors our outlook and makes us suspicious or skeptical of achievement. It is a condition in need of remedy." Rascoe particularly disliked critics who judged a work of art by comparing it with another, past work of art: "Comparisons are, after all, only a lazy man's easy method of getting out of work. It is much easier to say a new novel has points in common with a familiar one than to explain and illuminate these points as though they had never been thought of before. And it is much easier to say a new book

is a bad imitation of a well-known classic than it is to find reasons
for the inferiority. The trick is ancient. Caesar's characterization
of Plautus as 'a lesser Menander' is a familiar example. George
Jean Nathan's label for Maeterlinck, 'the Belgian Madam Blavat-
sky,' is a witty one. This is a method, however, which puts the
mind in the way of understanding rather than performing the
service of specific instruction."[32]

The need, as Rascoe saw it, was for more (but better) subjective criticism:

> ... If criticism is to be written, and I think it highly important
> that it should, it is inevitable that it be the reflection of idiosyn-
> crasies of taste, experience and criteria of judgment. But criticism
> does not need to be stupid or worthless on that account. It may
> be personal and yet based upon an understanding of the problem
> before the artist and an appreciation of the manner in which he
> resolved it. It may be subjective without revealing a tight and
> arid mind into which an unfamiliar idea or image could not be
> introduced by trepanning. And it may be, as it has often been,
> quite as valid a creative work as any other form of literary or
> artistic endeavor, in witness whereto we recall the "Poetics" of
> Aristotle and the critical work of Quintilian, Dryden, Coleridge,
> Hazlitt, Sainte-Beuve, Goethe, Arnold, Pater, Rémy de Gourmont,
> Anatole France and Sir Arthur Quiller-Couch, to name only a
> few.[33]

IV *Varieties of Criticism: Portraits and Satire*

Using his personal and impressionistic methods and style,
Rascoe achieved a reputation as a writer of biographical-critical
portraits. He wrote portraits of many of his contemporaries, and
they are among his best and most original contributions to criticism. Clarence Day wrote that "It is Mr. Rascoe's gift for written
portraits that I most admire him. He paints the wrinkle in a man's
liver, the wings of his brain."[34] And Lewis Galantière wrote enthusiastically to him about his portrait of E. E. Cummings: "The
A & D [*Arts and Decoration*] piece is a perfect wonder! How you
were ever able to remember just what Cummings said is something I shall never be able to understand. . . . It's a marvelous tour
de force, and you have all my admiration. Nobody could doubt
that this is his very self, and nobody who knows him could fail
to recognize him, even if he had been unnamed. This stuff ought

to make one of the great chapters of the book—.... You ask if I think you have done what you set out to do. I should say so! Cummings, in your own phrase, 'comes alive.' "[35]

Rascoe's portrait of Carl Sandburg in 1924 was one of the first extensive studies of Sandburg the poet and his work; a small portion of that portrait reads:

> So great, indeed, has been his success during the past three years that his innumerable and varied social contacts will inevitably wash away every vestige of his reforming temper and conquer his distress over social and economic conditions. More and more his poetry is becoming fanciful, imagistic and elegiac. Hitherto he has sung mostly one dolorous tune with numerous variations; he has sung the imminence of death and the ironic futility of human endeavor; and he has bidded men be kind to one another. He is growing less and less the protester against the social order and more and more the painter and etcher with a special, impressive vision....
>
> . . . .
>
> When he sets down his impressions, they are poetic and curious, but they might just as well apply to one thing as another, for they are not concrete. He wrote a prose poem about [Constantin] Brancusi, describing him as a "galoot," and wrote that Brancusi doesn't "know where is is going, but is on the way." He mixes slang, colloquialisms and Middle Western idioms into his poems with great effectiveness.
>
> Sandburg has the most deficient critical sense of any writer I know. He is a man almost entirely of intuitions about which he is more or less inarticulate. That accounts for much of the charm and impressiveness of his best poems. If he had a keener discrimination, a finer sense of word values and more general information —in a word, if he were more sophisticated—he would not display that genius for inappropriate analogy which makes the line "Shovel 'em in!" in his poem, "Cool Tombs," and the whole poem ["To a Contemporary Bunkshooter"] directed against Billy Sunday so startlingly distinctive....
>
> . . . .
>
> In Sandburg's poetry this confused critical sense becomes a shining virtue. Suggestion rather than explicit delineation and exposition is, of course, frequently the function of the highest poetry. And Sandburg's poetry usually intimates, or gives the impression of intimating, much more than what you see before your eyes when you read him. What he intimates, when you come right down to it, is that soon or late we are all going to die.[36]

Lew Sarett of Northwestern University wrote to Rascoe about this portrait: "Your article in the 'Lit. Rev.' on Carl Sandburg is a rattling good piece of work, so good that it moves me to knock off this note to tell you so. You 'got' Carl—something that few people succeed in doing—with all his human qualities, his peculiar slants, his spiritual tones; and, too, you've sensed the new direction of his growth in the past five years."[37]

As early as 1918, Guy Holt wrote to Rascoe: "You are, I believe, at your best in a controversy."[38] And it is true that some of Rascoe's best and most important work—editorial as well as critical—was the result of a controversy. He made—and he often said so—controversy his métier. His method in these critical battles was usually satire, reinforced with humor and irony. At its broadest, his satire became almost burlesque, as was, for example, his "review" in 1918 of Stuart Pratt Sherman's book, *On Contemporary Literature*, the opening paragraphs of which follow:

> Prof. Stuart Pratt Sherman, to propitiate Posterity, has rescued some of his brain children from the precarious orphanage of a weekly gazette, clothed them anew, fed them out of the generosity of his talent, and lodged them permanently in a domicile over the doorpost of which he has for some esoteric reason, inscribed the words *On Contemporary Literature* (Holt).
>
> We must cloak this act with the wings of our charity. That these children were conceived in error, that they are aberrant and defective, and that beauty and strength grace them not, should elicit our sympathy rather than our censure. Contrition is in the dedication, which is to Mr. Paul Elmer More; and atonement is in the frankness with which the author admits his dereliction. "I have been accused," says he, "of being a besotted mid-Victorian." *Oremus pro sibi.*
>
> It is unfortunate, of course, that these offspring should need bear names at all; but it is more so that Prof. Sherman was not more decorous in selecting them. The unhappy manner in which he cast about and filched prominent names must surely cause embarrassment. It were better, if such were possible, that these unfortunates might forego praenomens altogether, and answer simply to the name of Sherman. As it is, they, who might otherwise escape attention, draw curious eyes and painful comment.
>
> As a case in point: one wizened, emaciated, joyless creature, deeply serious in his pubescent preoccupation with the moral law, Prof. Sherman rather heartlessly burdens with the ludicrous

handle "The Aesthetic Naturalism of George Moore."...

. . . .

> Mr. Moore is sprightly of speech, engaging in conversation; the child is inarticulate and a stutterer. Mr. Moore is a Dionysian; the child is unnaturally concerned with hell fire and the rewards of the pure in heart. Mr. Moore is oblivious of anything that may be said for or against him; the child is morbidly sensitive, anxious to be thought nice, ambitious of being some day accepted in polite society.[39]

In the rest of this "review" Rascoe suggested that a better name for the chapter called "The Democracy of Mark Twain" would be "Wherein I Curry Favor with the Boston Back Bay Set," or "Wherein I Demonstrate Myself a Superior Person and a Conceited Prig"; and a better name for the chapter called "The Barbaric Naturalism of Theodore Dreiser" would be "Wherein I Convict Myself of Being One with the Unctuous Southey and the Clownish Lockhart, without the Wit of Either." Rascoe then hinted that, in "The Skepticism of Anatole France," Sherman had plagiarized from an essay by Lemaître. He concluded by suggesting that this brood of delinquent brainchildren of Sherman's be sterilized, "lest they propagate their kind and become a menace to our letters."

After this attack, Sherman and Rascoe continued sporadically to engage in critical feuds until Sherman's death in 1926. While Rascoe was associate editor of *Plain Talk*, he reviewed Jacob Zeitlin's and Homer Woodbridge's *Life and Letters of Stuart P. Sherman*. He said simply that

> I thought Mr. Sherman was wrong in condemning the work of Dreiser, Cabell, Mencken, Anderson, Lewisohn, George Moore, and almost the whole field of living writers who had given me great pleasure and had sustained me in my notion of the importance of life. What these writers had to say was not encouraging, to be sure; but to a young man, trying to earn a living as a journalist and finding life bewildering and severe, what they had to say steeled me in the business of living. Literature, it seemed to me, was a living thing, the product and expression of forces of life operating at the time of its writing. I subscribed then, as I do now, to the theory that there should be a free play of ideas. Let men have it out, but let us not have a face-stomping when the other man is strapped to the boards. It is not humane.[40]

The "face-stomping" referred to by Rascoe was Sherman's review of Mencken's *Prefaces* in *The Nation*, which had appeared during the war, and in which, Rascoe said, Sherman had viciously implied that Mencken was "in pay of Wilhelmstrasse."[41]

Later, when Rascoe was getting ready to publish his autobiography, *Before I Forget*, he sent Cabell the galley proofs to read. Cabell read them and advised Rascoe to delete the Rascoe-Zeitlin-Woodbridge correspondence about the Sherman book.[42] Rascoe's answer to Cabell was that ". . . Sherman *was* vicious and unscrupulous and the fact remains that the Zeitlin-Woodbridge two volume biography *does* contain slanderous matter about me that is based upon actual, provable lies by Sherman. It is true . . . that Sherman is very dead indeed, that he is mostly forgotten, and that few people besides myself have read the Zeitlin-Woodbridge biography; but it is also true that the Zeitlin-Woodbridge book is, and will be, regarded as a source book and it contains matter that is not true to the record." But he told Cabell that he would modify "the strictures on Sherman. Those strictures, however, are exactly how I felt and feel; for I believe him to have been essentially a dishonest person and a destructive force, and that if he were not consciously dishonest he had a monumental capacity to delude himself and never to doubt himself."[43] The next month he wrote to Cabell again, saying that ". . . I followed your advice and killed all of the correspondence about Sherman. You were right."[44]

In one of these letters to Zeitlin, Rascoe had explained his side of the feud with Sherman. He began his attacks upon Sherman, in his review of Sherman's *On Contemporary Literature*, because of Sherman's earlier review attacking Mencken's *A Book of Prefaces*. Sherman's review, Rascoe pointed out to Zeitlin, "was not merely an attack upon Mencken but an attack upon everyone who bore a German or a German-Jewish name . . . [and was] deliberately and consciously inciting the mob." And, "if Sherman was going to fight as dirty as that,[45] it was necessary to fight him dirty also or go yellow. . . ."[46] Consequently, Rascoe revealed to Zeitlin, he wrote *two* attacks on *On Contemporary Literature*, one in the *Chicago Tribune* and the other in the *Chicago Daily News*, "writing the News attack under the name Tom Reidy at the invitation of my rival editor, Henry Blackman Sell."[47]

V *Rascoe as a Stylist*

Rascoe wrote all of his critical appreciations and literary studies as a stylist—spontaneously, incautiously, explosively. But like any artist, he had his own style; his was influenced by the other literary radicals—especially by Mencken—but it was still strongly personal. He was fresh, unaffected, and original in his images and metaphors, sometimes even memorably brilliant; and he had a swift, fluid cadence. These aspects of his style can be seen in the beginning sentence of his review of Joris-Karl Huysmans's *A Rebours*: "This is the book that launched a thousand quips and burnt the topless towers of tedium"; and in the conclusion of this review:

> This is the first time that "A Rebours" has been [translated but] Mr. Howard's translation is superbly and sympathetically done. It comes a little late, perhaps too late, to find favor among the literate and literary youngsters. The fashion has changed. The aesthetic attitude is flouted by the Da-da-ists and Expressionists. Verlaine proclaimed himself the "empire at the close of the Decadence," and he might well have added, "après moi le déluge." The shimmering, soft beauty built by delicate precisions out of satyriasis and sick nerves has been chased across the horizon by a lusty pack of gibbering, irreverent and hilarious youths who grew so bored by the whispered awe of art on the part of the uncreative followers of the Decadence that they began to thumb their noses at art and tickle its ribs back into some show of animation. Already, though, Romains, Carco and other *Whitmanistes* in France are applying the glandular treatment to French poetry in an effort to give it a semblance of hairy-chested, gruff-voiced virility and succeeding in being but falsetto Sandburgs. But it shows the swing of the circle. Perhaps in another fifty years "A Rebours" will be treasured with as great affection as young men of the '90s brought to it. With them it was a red-lettered Bible, and like the other Bible, it was unfortunately cherished by many of them as a guide to conduct instead of an exquisite and entertaining bit of literature.[48]

Rascoe usually expressed his attitudes and judgments about writers and literature in the forms of critical humor, irony, parody, or satire; because of his personal methods of criticism, he considered his own style as resembling that "of Dekker, Swift, and Hazlitt or of any of the stylistic hoodlums of English literature."[49]

In *Titans*, for example, he described the French Academy as "that ornate and ribald sepulcher of mediocre talents" and its members as "correct and orthodox rhetoricians, a sterile and emasculate body of well-meaning mutual back-scratchers" who were, he said, "grim grammarians and concocters of pot-boilers who formed that areopagus of arid minds."[50] He described how successful was Flaubert's mistress, Mme Louise Colet, "who apparently had made up her mind to become, in turn, the mistress of all of the foremost literary men of her time."[51] Then he added ironically: "It is a satisfaction to all right-thinkers to learn that with age and experience and vanished good looks Mme Colet's character was refined and that she achieved high moral standards and an intolerance of evil."[52] He satirized Henry James and his style by parody. James, he wrote, "shook the dust from a 'vulgar' America and removed himself to England, where through a long period he braced English aristocratic society and, in novels, gave a profound psychological significance to the manner in which a duchess accepted a cup of tea from a younger, remote cousin of a son of a man with whom she had had, in her dim past, an irregular affair."[53] Both the excellencies and the deficiencies of his style are apparent in this method of criticism. At his best, his style is of a very high order and perhaps is of more lasting value than his critical judgments, many of which have become the standard ones. At Rascoe's worst, chiefly because of his haste in writing for deadlines and because of the huge quantity of work he did, he too often rambles and becomes incoherent or repetitious; his images, metaphors, and similes are sometimes grotesque, in poor taste, or trite; his sentences are sometimes so long that they are almost impossible to follow; and his impressions are sometimes vague thinking—although the thinking is always directed toward something that is not vague.

Implicit, then, in all of Rascoe's writings and in his editorial work—his literary battles and appreciations, his biographical-literary criticism, his autobiographies, his histories of ideas, even his anti-communist articles of the 1930's and 1940's—was his essentially Romantic set of values in life and art. Lewis Galantière, in a letter to Rascoe about *Before I Forget*, pointed out the extent and consequences of this Romanticism in Rascoe's life:

... one reason why you understand Sherwood Anderson so well
is that your America and his are both XIXth Century America,

whereas by contrast Red Lewis's is already XXth Century America. Sherwood's questionings are different to Red's; he asks himself about Man; Red about Society; and you too asked in [*Before I Forget*] yourself about Man. ... what is specifically American in your book ... is the concern with mystery in a pioneer world, a world [now] wholly given over to a concern with material building. ... it was that concern, and not any conscious ambition, which of itself shaped your career; your goal was and is spiritual, though the road you have taken to reach it be, in the nature of things material (your family have to live.) [54]

And in another letter to Rascoe, Galantière pointed out that spiritual goals had determined Rascoe's life and career as a literary editor and critic: "... your dreams were never of yourself but of philosophy (relation of self to the universe, requiring therefore some acquaintance with an understanding of the universe). Your career, clearly, made itself by virtue of an inner compulsion not concerned with a career at all, but concerned with things totally immaterial." [55]

CHAPTER 3

Manning the Critical Barricades:
1917-1932

R ASCOE DID his most original and most important work between 1917 and 1932—from his earliest spirited defense of
James Branch Cabell until his publication of *Titans of Literature*,
perhaps his best book. As an editor and a critic during this time,
he contributed importantly to the outcome of some of the most
important critical and literary controversies that occurred during
this period; and he wrote some of the earliest, most significant
and perceptive critical judgments about some of his contemporary
writers and critics.

I *In Defense of James Branch Cabell*

Rascoe first reviewed a book by Cabell on December 29, 1917;
in this review of *The Cream of the Jest* Rascoe asserted that "No
first rate writer in the history of our literature has suffered so
much neglect as Cabell."[1] Essentially, his review was, as he said
later in *Before I Forget*, "an impassioned exhortation to the reading public to treat themselves to this book which had given me
so much pleasure."[2] In his "exhortation" Rascoe argued that
Cabell's neglect—Cabell had been writing novels since 1902 but
with little critical success—was caused mainly by "reviewers who
damn books without reading them, and [by] critics who do not
know a piece of literature when they see one." There was one
exception, however, that Rascoe noted: "H. L. Mencken, the only
discerning and hospitable critic since Huneker left the field of
combat, is the only reviewer who, it seems, has read and enjoyed
the book."[3]

To Rascoe this neglect of Cabell was a paradigm of what was
wrong with this country, and he decided to try to correct this
wrong. To Cabell he wrote: "I wish to assure you, Mr. Cabell,

that if my humble typewriter can acquire a potency it does not now possess, it shall help to make your own name known among the discerning readers of this genial but ingenuous republic."⁴ Several months later he told Cabell again, "I shall mention you almost every week," and he added, "The Tribune readers are already beginning to become familiar with your name, at least."⁵ Beginning on February 18, 1918, he ran weekly selections from Cabell's *Beyond Life* in the *Tribune*, using almost all of the book. Rupert Hughes read these selections and, in a long letter to Rascoe, attacked Cabell's Greek and medieval inaccuracies and "historical blunders.'"⁶ Rascoe then engineered a literary fight between Hughes and Cabell, knowing full well the news value of such a battle; and on April 27, May 4, May 11, and May 18 he published Cabell-Hughes exchanges.⁷

In this campaign to win recognition for Cabell, Rascoe denounced in angry letters the Chicago critics who ignored or attacked Cabell's work—among whom were Ben Hecht, Keith Preston, Riquarius (Richard Atwater), and the visiting Englishman, Robert Nichols. He also wrote several deliberately controversial articles about Cabell's work in which he compared Cabell to Stevenson, Lamb, Pater, Congreve, Gautier, France, and Molière. Rascoe was immediately attacked for writing these articles, as he knew and hoped he would be. Lewis Galantière wrote to warn Rascoe that his estimate of Cabell was "too rash, too hasty"; and Galantière quoted for Rascoe's benefit Sainte-Beuve's "It is of this difficult tomorrow that every serious artist must think." He also censured Rascoe for comparing Cabell's prose style with Stevenson's.⁸

Rascoe argued with Galantière, maintaining that Cabell was Stevenson's "equal in prose style and superior to him in intelligence and creative ability." And about Sainte-Beuve Rascoe said:

> It has escaped your mind for a moment, Lewis, that Sainte-Beuve was a journalist, a newspaperman like Percy Hammond or myself even—he had to do a regular stint of book reviewing or he couldn't eat. . . . Sainte-Beuve was not half so interested in "that difficult tomorrow" as he was . . . in getting a review off his hands as expeditiously as possible that he might be with Mme Hugo all the longer—or with some other dame who had fallen for him. The great French critic? *The* great critic of his century? All right, I agree with you—but a human being, certainly, and not

the Holy Ghost. Let's you and I, if no one else in the world ever does, get away from holding our breaths and keeping our mouths open when a great name is mentioned: . . . [let us not be] too ready to fall down before a hierarchy of literary names; [let us not be] ready to regard certain writers as inviolate, inviolable, immaculate, and unmentionable in comparison.[9]

That the writers of the past were only human beings was Rascoe's chief contention, and he thought that they should be regarded as such. And, by January, 1920, so many articles of critical acclaim had been written about Cabell—one had just appeared in *The Smart Set,* another in *The Atlantic*—that Rascoe felt not only that his fight was over, but that he had been victorious. To Cabell he wrote: "It is pleasant and soul-satisfying to see all this jubilant vindication by eminent personages of the convictions I had and have about you and over which I fought with such ire and bitterness." He told Cabell that next he might do battle with Stuart Sherman:

> I must take some time and care in disposing of Paul Elmer More and Stuart Sherman. Did you see Sherman's marvellous assassination of Mencken in The Times? It was really an excellent piece of work, even down to his pinking me. I wrote him a letter of congratulation, and told him I was polishing my poniard. Sherman can write. If it weren't for his slavish adoration of the Calvinistic Paul Elmer More and his belief that a critic must take a high moral tone, he would be a great critic. As it is, he believes one thing, I think, and expresses another. My admiration for him since his assault on Mencken is the admiration of any good sportsman for a worthy antagonist. He was Nietzschean, Prussian, unethical, in his determination to draw blood. His defense was wretched and vulnerable, but he prevented notice of it by his brilliant attack. He is an enemy worth having and worth cultivating.[10]

But the Cabell battle was not won; before the end of the month, Rascoe found himself involved in a bitter feud with Conrad Aiken over the merits of Cabell.

II   *Feuding with Aiken*

His feud with Aiken—with whom he had corresponded for years—began with Rascoe's review of Aiken's *Scepticisms,* which appeared on Rascoe's "Saturday Page" of the *Tribune* on January

31, 1920. In this review Rascoe attacked Aiken as a critic but defended him as a poet. Aiken, who was furious, wrote an article for *The Athenaeum* in which he attacked Cabell's *Jurgen,* which had been dedicated to Rascoe; and he wrote Rascoe three angry letters. In the first of these letters, written on February 17, Aiken criticized Rascoe for his "disposition to fatuous excesses"; in the second, written the next day, he described Rascoe's review of *Scepticisms* as "lying and filth"; and in the third, written two days later, he denounced Rascoe for his "dishonest[y] and bad taste" in the *Scepticism* review, and said that Rascoe's attack was motivated by his disagreeing with Rascoe over Cabell's *Jurgen*.[11]

Rascoe answered Aiken on March 2, admitting the motivation, and saying that Aiken's review was a "barbouillage," that it could have made difficult the negotiations for "the disposal of the English rights to Cabell's book," and that it might have had the "effect of sicking on the smut hounds" on *Jurgen*. He then explained more clearly his objections to Aiken's *Scepticisms*:

> . . . you postulate a perfect critic which you urge me to aspire to, which, if you will pardon me, makes me laugh. I have no desire to become this bewhiskered fraud you reverence so obtusely. I quite frankly champion men whose work I like and lean away from men whose work I do not like. Your gabble about "speculative inquiry" and "perception of the absolute relativity of values" is, to my mind, the apotheosis of critical nonsense, a symptom of the delusion of infallibility. If, to paraphrase Anatole France, you think that in "Scepticisms" you are doing anything more than showing up yourself and exposing your prejudices, you are thinking through your hat. It seems, indeed, that before sending your "speculative inquiries" to press a suspicion of this trickled into your superbly hermetic consciousness. How otherwise account for your "Apologia Pro Specie Sua"? No, your "speculative inquiries" and such twaddle must go by the boards to join M. Brunetière's lamented "objective criticism."

Rascoe then explained not only his point of view in this feud but also his view of the role of the critic:

> To harp back upon my over-enthusiasms, let me urge upon you my conviction that it is a critic's duty to discover new authors, provide as adequately as possible an audience for them, to dispense praise, even overpraise, when merit is obvious, and to insure a laudation while he is yet alive. . . . It is a satisfaction

always to me to salute a new figure or a new book in which I thoroughly and honestly believe. That, I believe, is what I am hired for; that and to deal heavy blows upon the heads of self-seeking individuals who wish to gain notice for themselves by attacking him. If you will recall, my severe attacks have always been leveled against critics, not against poets or novelists or essayists; against Stuart Pratt Sherman, against [Edgar] Jepson, [Louis] Untermeyer, against [W. C.] Brownell, against yourself.

That, too, is a delusion of yours, Conrad—that idea that a critic should or can direct the work of another writer. A critic's adumbrations are—or should be—addressed to the public; if they are intended for the author, a private letter would suffice and would be in better taste. Do you suppose for a moment I thought that my attacks on Sherman would alter his way of thinking or writing? Not at all. I wrote to discredit in the eyes of as many as I could reach those ideas which seemed to be pernicious to art, fallacious, and even dangerous to literary freedom.

The rest of the letter was a defense of Rascoe's appreciations and of his type of personal criticism:

"Jurgen" gives me immensely more personal pleasure than the "Divine Comedy": and . . . I shall probably read it innumerably more times than I shall read "Hamlet." You see, you cautious critics who tremble before tradition as if you were in the Presence, and shrink before great names as if they were all Jahweh, cannot believe your ears when you hear the blasphemy of us impetuous ones, and take pains to soften it when you repeat it. Thus the legend has come down that [Honoré-Gabriel Riqueti] Mirbeau [sic] merely called [Maurice] Maeterlinck the Belgian Shakespeare. His actual words were: "M. Maeterlinck a donné l'oeuvre la plus géniale de ce temps, et la plus extra-ordinaire et le plus naïve aussi, comparable—et oserai—je le dire?—supérieure in beauté a ça qu'il y a de plus beau dans Shakespeare." . . . I happen to disagree with Mirbeau [sic] but I honor him for his honesty and his enthusiasm all the more. After all, he may be right; certainly, it is not for you or for me to say definitely and finally that he is not.[12]

III   Rascoe's Early Essential Mencken

Rascoe's long correspondence with Mencken began in 1914. During the war he wrote to Mencken: "I believe in you as I believe in few men. . . . I am tremendously pleased to hear about your plans for a monthly journal. After the war we are going to need such intellects as yours to counteract on the one hand the vitiating propaganda of the *Haszgesang gegen Deutchland* and on the other the more demoralizing shouting for democracy of bunk prophets. You are singularly equipped for the work. Even now I am carrying your name into the waste places, slaying foes, and getting converts."[13] On November 6, 1917, Rascoe wrote to Mencken that he was using a "Fanfare" review of Mencken's *A Book of Prefaces* on his Saturday "highbrow page." This review, which he told Mencken had been rejected by *Vanity Fair*, appeared in the Chicago *Tribune* on November 11, 1917; and it is significant—it is sound, comprehensive, and illuminating, and it is particularly admirable in that it was the first lengthy article to appear anywhere about Mencken.[14]

In "Fanfare" Rascoe made the point that Mencken should first be considered as an artist, not as a literary critic, because he had the true mark of a stylist: "an aptitude for connotation" and a varied vocabulary. Rascoe then added: "His vivid combinations, his apt coinage of words are traceable to a close observation and appraisement of daily affairs. Add a nimble imagination and you have the recipe of his style, the most vigorous and individual in this country. It is the style of a satirist and humorist of a high order, who is equal to compact and devastating expletives such as 'the jitney geniuses of Washington Square' and 'the kept idealists of the New Republic.'. . . It moves with an irregular tempo, replete with Wagnerian dissonances. It is imagistic, colorful, dynamic." But, Rascoe explained,

> Mencken has his share of intellectual fourflush. . . . He has a habit of uttering glib dicta regarding men about whose work it is evident he knows nothing and a vainglorious trick of parading names of unfamiliar writers through the pages of his discourse, . . .
>
> He has an intolerance as definite in its way as the intolerance of the Methodism and Puritanism he fights. . . . At heart he is a Puritan, as was Nietzsche and is Shaw.
>
> And he has his regular fling at bourgeoisie baiting, a pastime he pleasingly alternates with badgering the "intellectuals." It is great fun for him. With an adjective and a noun he can strip a Chautauqua pundit of every stitch of his pretentious accouterments and leave him shivering in the altogether, a pathetic and ridiculous spectacle.

He is at best as a critic, of course, in dealing with prose literature. He has little patience with or appreciation for poetry and
with characteristic impromptu he is likely to consign to the
limbo of his estimates along with a hack versifier a poet of high
caliber, whose methods and aims he does not immediately apper-
ceive. It is this intolerance, these snap and final judgments, this
childish delight in an occasional display of cultural bijouterie,
that lessen his stature as a critic. Some of us hope that before
long he will shed this impedimenta and gain a trifle more of poise
and balance, without losing thereby his gem-like quality of
phrase. . . .[15]

"Fanfare" was appreciative but caustic; and, considering that
it was written in 1917, it has proved amazingly accurate in its
judgments. William Manchester in his biography of Mencken
praised Rascoe for his courage in writing "Fanfare"; Manchester
noted that Mencken's *Prefaces*

received only three favorable notices, and one was from the
Socialist *New York Call,* itself suspected of treason. The other
two were in the loyal *Boston Transcript* and Burton Rascoe's book
page in the *Chicago Tribune.* In the light of what later happened,
Rascoe's piece is significant. It was by far the most forceful of the
three; it appeared, under the three-column etched head "Fanfare," at a time when to speak out as it did was dangerous; it was
the first indication that Mencken's work had penetrated beyond
the Atlantic coast. Rascoe reviewed the whole range of Mencken's
work to date, stuck himself far out on the limb in echoing the
book's sentiments, and wrote of "a bellicose extravagance, arising
to meet a peculiariarly American need." The rare character of
the review was reflected in a touching letter of thanks from
Mencken:[16] . . . Rascoe followed his review with a terrific blast at
Sherman. . . .[17]

This "terrific blast" was Rascoe's satirical review of Sherman's *On
Contemporary Literature.* In 1919, Mencken asked for Rascoe's
permission to reprint "Fanfare" in pamphlet form.[18] Mencken
supplied Rascoe with some biographical data, and Rascoe ex-
panded his original article for the pamphlet.

On March 4, 1922—shortly after Rascoe had become literary
editor of the *New York Tribune*—his second important article on
Mencken appeared in "The Literary Review" of the *New York
Evening Post*: "Notes for an Epitaph: H. L. Mencken." In this

long article Rascoe reviewed Mencken's work and influence, evaluating it as being extremely important; but he also showed that
Mencken had become accepted, approved of, and quoted everywhere; that he had been "brought into the line of regimented
thought"; and that he had become "respectable," leaving the
youth of America without an "agitator." After pointing out
Mencken's vast influence over the young writers throughout
America, Rascoe commented on Mencken's deficiencies as a critic.
This long article, it seems to me, shows Rascoe at his best as a
stylist and as an evaluator; it is, therefore, worth quoting at
length:

... it is not as a literary critic, I think, that Mencken's fame will
survive. He has had the misfortune not to keep up with the literary tendencies to which he directed attention. And he lacks a
background of catholic culture which is so necessary for a broad
critical understanding. There is meagre evidence in the whole
body of his critical work that he has read any book published
before 1880. With the cultural heritage of all nations, excepting
only the English Bible, he reflects little intimacy. And while one
can easly forgive him for not knowing Homer and Shakespeare,
the Greeks and the Latins, Balzac and Dostoievsky, one cannot
forgive him in the role of critic for being inordinately proud of
this ignorance. It is difficult to accept his assurance that because
he has not read them they are therefore one and all "geysers of
pishposh."
  Moreover, Mencken is too conservative in his literary judgments to satisfy a growing audience in this country with catholic
taste and inquisitive habits of mind. It is not to his discredit—
indeed, it is in the interest of consistency—that his championings
have almost invariably been for ethical ideas rather than for
literary values; but this tendency has colored his opinions very
luridly in some instances, notably concerning W. L. George.[19]
His bias for books has been towards those which reflect a defiance
of Puritanism and a distrust of the principle of democracy; but
even in this he is lately disposed to call a halt. "Three Soldiers"
shocked him a bit and "Erik Dorn" left him somewhat discon-
certed.
  The truth is that the literary generation now gaining recognition has progressed beyond the reaches of Mencken's aesthetic
equipment. His first chill reception of Sherwood Anderson, his
first antagonism against the modern poets which led him to make
that unforgettable reference to Alfred Kreymborg as a "cheap-

jack," his original lukewarm attitude towards so many writers who have since been accepted as having high merit, have combined to force him to climb upon the band wagon who was once a leader of the band.

On the ideational side Mencken has, I believe, much yet to give. On the aesthetic side he had not much to give in the first place. A fascinated pupil at the feet of Huneker and Percival Pollard, he left his classes with a handy list of romantic names, but with an actual interest in only such of them as had, for him, a definite sociological, ethical, or political significance, i. e., Nietzsche, Shaw, Ibsen, and Brieux. He showed from the first makings of an excellent satirico-political irritant rather than of an appraiser of beauty.[20] He is a logical and analytical, not a sensitive man. He has unquestionably an intuitive appreciation for that which is fine and honest in prose composition, particularly if it reflects in a measure his own attitude towards life. But he has remained insensitive to almost the entire reach of lyrical or ecstatic expression, whether it be in prose literature, painting, music, or poetry. He admires homiletic and pamphleteering prose, i.e., prose that is clear, concise, direct, and a little flashy; but with writing considered as an art in itself, as an instrument of feeling, nuance, and suggestion, he has little patience. If the ideas behind a prose style are vaguely consonant with his own he makes valiant effort to commend the manner also. The result, sometimes, is amusing, particularly if he offers favorable comment upon the caviar. "He knows where a red noun should go and where a peacock-blue verb, and where an adjective as darkly purple as a grape. He is an imagist in prose." So he wrote recently of Cabell.

It is very funny, of course, to see Mencken talking through the hat that belongs to René Ghil;[21] but it is the second sentence which gives away his misapprehension of, or distaste for, graceful methods of expression. Cabell's style is the furthest removed from the imagistic. It might be said of Hergesheimer, for instance, that he is at times an imagist; but Cabell is occupied not at all with outlines and surfaces. He is more accurately described as a symbolist; he is subjective and suggestive, seldom objective and decorative. It is this defective sense of word arrangements, his lack of sympathy with "writing," which has been responsible for [Mencken's] grating ineptitudes about the work of Henry James, Robert Browning, Conrad Aiken, E. A. Robinson, Robert Frost, and many another who has striven for a precision and subtlety which is neither blatant nor baldly obvious.

. . . .

... even towards that literature which Mencken seems to feel the most he adopts a clinical air of pert sophistication which fails fully to illuminate or to carry conviction. His stock stamp, "He gets into his pages a genuine bounce and gusto," which he uses on books varying widely in manner and content, is about as much as he has to say in elucidation of a writer's aim and achievements. It is not that he does not feel deeply, but that his emotions are primarily sentimental and not aesthetic, and, being a sentimental fellow, he has built up a defense mechanism of gay cynicism which stands between him and a free expression of the emotion felt and recorded. He gave up verse after his first love affair and thereafter firmly believed that poets never wrote anything except moon-shiny nonsense, and even late in life he made the assertion that no good poetry was ever written after a poet had reached twenty. It is much nearer the truth to say that no good poetry was ever written by any one under twenty-five. He has probably never taken the trouble to enter the Metropolitan Museum, so he characterizes it as a "storehouse of rubbish." He has been too busy to investigate the development of music since Brahms, so he says all modern music is so much caterwauling. He is too much occupied to find out what the modern poets are doing, so he says their work is all hogwash.[22]

In the rest of this long essay Rascoe went on to conclude that Mencken's ideas about and attitudes toward the arts were essentially no different from those of the man in the street, who, as soon as he learns what Mencken has said, "will see to it that Mencken is made a classic, read in the schools, that he gets into the Academy, ..." Certainly, Rascoe said, Mencken's having been "so vital and human a force" was a great accomplishment; and the "deficiencies in Mencken's critical make-up are doubtless the tax one must pay for the ground clearing work he has done." Yet Rascoe stated that he was glad that Mencken "has forfeited his drum-majorship with the young révoltés," because perhaps his greatest work—his *magnum opus*—still lay before him, since he was then only in his early forties.

Many people read and commented on this article. Vincent Starrett picked Rascoe to succeed Mencken; he wrote: "In a recent fulmination entitled 'Notes for an Epitaph,' Burton read the service over his old friend Mencken . . . , and found occasion to say: 'Now that Mencken is become respectable, the literary youth of America is suddenly bereft of an agitator.' . . . Yes, Burton himself must be Mencken's successor; I think the literary youth referred to will vote for Rascoe, a better critic than Mencken anyway, and probably as efficient an agitator when he gets his hand in."[23]

Joel E. Spingarn, who was enthusiastic about the article, wrote to tell Rascoe so the very next day:

I simply must tell you how much I liked your article on Mencken in last night's *Evening Post*. It had all the vigor that has been put into out literature in the Mencken Era, but with a sense of the finer distinctions that were in danger of coming to an end (or transformed), and I now foresee a new spirit of which your article gives at least a hint. But I wonder if the youth of the future need merely more revolt, except in so far as all of us must forever rebel against dry rot and the worship of dead idols. The rest of the world is beginning to tire of revolt for revolt's sake; America has had a dozen years of it (and heaven knows it was needed). But what we need now is rather a new aesthetic and a spiritual *faith*, not drawn from the past but created afresh by ourselves. I should like to talk these things over with you some day.[24]

Alfred Kreymborg wrote later that month from Pallanza, Italy, saying that he had just read "The Literary Review" "with your superb oration on Mencken. ... The article on the whole was positively the sort of thing we need now, straight, brave, clear-visioned criticism. It gave me a pang to think that you haven't a column somewhere in New York to give us some more of the same. And then some more. I believe I know better than any other, how poignantly New York needs a Chicagoan to hammer away at its smug, sneaking backwoods imbecility. Hell on earth, does McCall's take all your time? And the novel?"[25] Kreymborg in Italy had not yet learned of Rascoe's being then with the *Tribune*.

Over two years later Mark Van Doren, editor of *The Nation*, remembered Rascoe's article and wrote to ask him to review Mencken's *Prejudices*. Van Doren commented: "All of his [Mencken's] talk about a new departure and so forth reminds me of your 'epitaph,' and it seems to me that you are just the man to take the measure of H. L.'s new subject matter."[26]

Subsequent critics writing on Mencken have merely reiterated much of what Rascoe said in these two articles.[27] For example, late in 1922 Newton Arvin was stimulated by Rascoe's "Epitaph" to write an essay on Mencken in which he said:

> Early in the spring Mr. Burton Rascoe wrote for the *Literary Review* an article on Mr. Mencken, entitled, "Notes for an Epitaph." [The article was] critical and saline, but, upon the whole, encomiastic; . . . Mr. Rascoe was entirely right, however, in treating Mr. Mencken with some finality, for his work is no longer in his formative stages, and the publication of the third series of "Prejudices" serves only to remind us that he is by this time a recognized national figure, perhaps our first man of the "literary dictator" type. And at least tentative evaluation is surely not out of order, and it seems to me we need to clear our minds a little about Mr. Mencken and his rôle. The importance of that rôle no one has exaggerated; but the nature of it, I think, is widely misunderstood. I mean that Mr. Mencken is most commonly looked upon as a literary critic, and, whatever else he is, it seems to me he is not that, in any strict sense, at all. He falls short of being a true literary critic because of certain serious defects of equipment, of temper, and of insight.
>
> The first of these—his defects of equipment—is perhaps the least important, yet surely it is not one to be left out of account. Mr. Rascoe himself points out that there is nothing in Mr. Mencken's work to indicate a real familiarity with any author previous to 1880, or with any of the great English classic except the Bible and Shakespeare.[28]

Arvin concluded in his article that "What [Mencken] really is, is a social critic, and besides that, a humorist of a very high order"; and "it is as a humorist, I think, that he may most justly be considered"; for Mencken was not "literary-minded" and had "no taste for poetry."[29] But Arvin was not saying anything new; five years earlier in "Fanfare" Rascoe had said the same thing and in almost the same words: "It is the style [Mencken's] of a satirist and humorist of a very high order. . . ." And two years before Arvin's article, Rascoe had sent F. Scott Fitzgerald a copy of the *Fanfare* pamphlet; and Fitzgerald had written to Rascoe about it on November 17, 1920: "Thanks for the pamphlet[.] I enjoyed your essay on Mencken—I think its [sic] a clever touch: his 'being the only true American,' just as Anatole France 'is the only living Catholic.' Also I agree with you that he is a great man and bum critic of poetry."

IV *Undermining the "Algonquin" Influence*

One of Rascoe's many objectives as literary editor of the *New York Tribune* was to undermine the "pernicious" cultural influence of the "Algonquin group" (Heywood Broun, Franklin P. Adams, and Alexander Woollcott) by exposing their "pretensions and their enthusiasms for trivial writers and trivial notions."[30] In his attempt to do so, he reviewed in 1922 A. S. M. Hutchinson's new book, *This Freedom,* because Hutchinson was a favorite writer of this group. Rascoe's review was vitriolic, but he was really attacking the "Algonquins." He pointed out that Hutchinson was a wretched writer of English and a "third-rate journeyman . . . whom injudicial critical opinion has, somehow, hoisted into the ridiculous position of a claimant to literary homage." He analyzed Hutchinson's style, showing that it "was dull, wooden and stilted." A man of genius might survive such bad writing, Rascoe noted, giving examples; but "In Mr. Hutchinson it is not possible to divert one's attention from the cheap and flash prose hand-me-downs because the personality behind them is so commonplace and ineffectual." Rascoe then made clear the purpose of his attack; he said that he would not be pointing out these inadequacies of Mr. Hutchinson's if he "had not, probably against his will and ambition, been urged upon his audience not as an entertainer, a writer of ephemeral novels, but as a literary artist."[31] After this review, Rascoe said, Broun, Adams, and Woollcott were silent; they had "apparently crossed Hutchinson off their list."[32]

Rascoe similarly ridiculed Zane Grey's *Wanderer of the Wasteland* in 1923, and concluded that the book was immoral in the code of conduct it expounded. He said that he reviewed it only because of the large reading audience commanded by the novel and that he did not believe that any literary editor with any sense of responsibilities to his readers could afford to ignore the achievement of such an audience; and "I flatter myself that I have a proper sense of these responsibilities."[33] But in 1956 in the typescript (BRC) of his unpublished "Chicago's Golden Age in Life and Letters," under the "Rascoe" entry, he wrote that he later regretted that he had spent so much time and energy on such reviews—which he had first started writing in Chicago. He explained that it had been his policy in Chicago to give notice to the new works by popular writers, not by reviewing them himself but by delegating attention to the best-selling lists, and to the works of popular romantic fiction, to Fannie Butcher. Rascoe did exert himself rather foolishly to what he intended to be a "devastating" article analyzing one of Zane Grey's novels, "Wildfire" (1917), showing that the author, though heavily moralistic in tone and in fact, had propounded a moral problem and had solved it in a palpably immoral and unethical way. The article was quoted *in extenso* in the New York Literary Digest, which devoted a whole page of the magazine to it. But it was an analysis which would be interesting to nobody except those who wouldn't think of reading a Zane Grey novel in the first place. It did not lessen Zane Grey's clientele of readers or damage his prestige any more than it had already been damaged by Grey himself and by literate reviewers everywhere. . . . Rascoe, also, acting on the presumption that there is a sort of Gresham's law operating in literature as well as in currency, whereby the bad tends to drive out the good, got into quite a youthful lather over a new novel, "Just David" (1916) by Mrs. Eleanor Porter, the creator of the Pollyanna series which gave a new word to the dictionaries, meaning offensively sweet, mawkish, and overly cheerful.

. . . [Later Rascoe was] ashamed that he had been so indignant, in print, about the sort of book that could only give comforting pleasure to the sort of people who enjoyed that kind of thing; for it was not the sort of book that could, say, drive out the sounder currency of novels by Willa Cather, Ellen Glasgow, or May Sinclair. . . .

V *Sponsorship of T. S. Eliot*

Another objective of Rascoe's was to publicize his own enthusiasms. He read, for example, Eliot's *The Waste Land* on October 26, 1922; and he wrote his impressions of it that day in his "Day Book," saying in part:

Received the November issue of the Dial today. It contains T. S. Eliot's new long poem, THE WASTE LAND, a thing of bitterness and beauty, which is a crystallization or a synthesis of all the poems Mr. Eliot has hitherto written. It is, perhaps, the finest poem of this generation; at all events it is the most significant in that it gives voice to the universal despair or resignation arising from the spiritual and economic consequences of the war, the cross purposes of modern civilzation, the cul-de-sac into which both science and philosophy seem to have got themselves and

the break-down of all great directive purposes which give zest
and joy to the business of living. It is an erudite despair: Mr.
Eliot stems his poem from a recent anthropological study of prim-
itive beliefs, as embodied in the Grail legend and other flaming
quests which quickened men in other times; he quotes, or mis-
quotes, lines from the Satyricon of Petronius, Tristan and Isolde,
the sacred books of the Hindus, Dante, Baudelaire, Verlaine,
nursery rhymes, the Old Testament and modern jazz songs. His
method is highly elliptical, based on the curious formula of Tristan Corbière, wherein reverential and blasphemous ideas are
juxtaposed in amazing antitheses, and there are mingled all the
shining verbal toys, impressions and catch lines of a poet who has
read voraciously and who possesses an insatiable curiosity about
life. It is analysis and realism, psychology and criticism, anguish,
bitterness and disillusion, with passages of great lyrical beauty.[34]

For months Rascoe defended Eliot's poem. He began one of
his "Day Book" columns, reprinted as "A Defense of T. S. Eliot"
in *A Bookman's Daybook*,[35] by observing that "Gilbert Seldes,
Edmund Wilson, Jr., and I made merry over the fact that here
were gathered together three critics looked upon as arch-conspir-
ators in the effort to palm off on the public an unintelligible poem
by an obscure scribbler as the great poetic work of the year."[36]
Rascoe then explicated part of the poem to show just how intelligible it really was. In another "Day Book" column Rascoe defended the poem against attacks by Louis Untermeyer. First,
Rascoe quoted a letter which Untermeyer had sent to him (here
quoted only in part): "I have no right to question your playing
Hamlet to Mr. Eliot ... but ... you take a perfectly dispassionate
article of mine on 'The Wasteland' (*sic*) and ... proceed to distort
my conclusions for the edification of the thousands to whom
Sundays means ... another Bookman's Day Book."

Untermeyer's letter listed the four points he had made in an
article and which Rascoe had criticized; points three and four
were: "That this work is not essentially a creative thing, but a
piece of carpentry; erudite joiner's work; the flotsam and jetsam
of dessicated culture stuck together in the puzzle-picture manner
of Pound's 'Sordello-form' cantos"; and "That a poem which relies
on the books of seven different languages, that points to thirty-
odd sources for its disjected quotations, that necessitates fifty
explanatory notes and reading of two works of anthropology to
... elucidate the difficulties of the poem'—such a man is not only

a retreat into literature but a confession of imaginative sterility."

Rascoe began his "answer" by spelling the title of the poem correctly. His last comment was about Untermeyer's fourth point: "But *does* the music of the Fifth Symphony actually depend upon the program notes, and, finally, *does* the poetry of 'The Waste Land' depend upon Mr. Eliot's jottings in explanation? Not in the least. Both sets of notes are of intellectual and literary interest, but they are no more necessary for the enjoyment of the essential poetry than are the variorum notes necessary for the enjoyment of Shakespeare's poetry. Mr. Eliot's anticipation of a subsidiary intellectual interest in his poem by appending some explanatory notes is, far from 'a confession of imaginative sterility,' rather an earnest of an unusually fecund imagination."[37]

VI *First Study of Dreiser*

Rascoe's first book, *Theodore Dreiser*, and the first book about Dreiser, was published in 1925.[38] In his own published copy of the book (BRC), he has struck out large portions of the material —some of the irrelevancies, some of the more polemic parts, and some of his earlier judgments. He has also made corrections in the diction, syntax, organization, and style. An examination of the structure shows, too, that part of the chapter on Dreiser's achievement was purely biographical and should have been included in the biographical section; that the book contained too many attacks on Dreiser's opponents—Stuart Pratt Sherman in particular —instead of critical analyses of Dreiser's works; and that it is not of much permanent critical value.

Except for the part showing that Dreiser was a consequence of the industrial development and some analyses of Dreiser's major works, the book shows evidence of being superficially and hastily written. Yet the book did have a certain extrinsic value: it was a forceful answer to some of the strictures of Sherman. In the book Rascoe analyzed Sherman's essay on Dreiser in *On Contemporary Literature;* and Rascoe ridiculed, attacked, and corrected Sherman, while defending Dreiser and his works; and he also attacked the other critics who had said that Dreiser's picture of life was false.

In a long review of Rascoe's book in the *New York Morning Telegraph,* on August 16, 1925, G. D. Eaton wrote that he had earlier muttered "regretful incantations over [Rascoe's] early grave," even as Rascoe had "buried" Mencken; but Eaton was "grateful to find that they were ... premature." With the publication of *Theodore Dreiser,* Rascoe

> has again captured the great admiration I felt for him when, as one of the pioneer critics, he was sniping at the trucklers who cluttered our literature to the exclusion of almost all honest and decent writers. I am again of the opinion that there is no critic in America who can write with the clearness and neatness, with his alert and swift summation.
>
> . . . .
>
> What deserves special mention is Rascoe's treatment of the evolution of present-day American fiction of the better sort. He has done this, I am convinced, better in a few pages than Carl Van Doren has done in a whole book. It reminds me that there is a big job on tap for Rascoe. He is obviously the man to handle the history of the literary revolt during the past seven or eight years.[39]

VII *Attack on New Humanism*

The literary group most active during the late 1920's was the anti-Romantic New Humanists. To Seward Collins, publisher and editor (after Rascoe) of *The Bookman,* Rascoe wrote a long letter in 1929 in which he announced his declaration of war on this group:

> You see, I do not by any means concede that the war has been won and the new Era of the New Humanism inaugurated just because you have announced this consummation in the Bookman. I have been reading very diligently among all its expositors and I have yet to find out what the New Humanism is. But I am pleased to see that you have been on the road to Damascus and that you are ready to proclaim the New Gospel (having foresworn all the old gods). You seem to have evolved a solid and vigorous program and to be prepared to pursue it with passionate enthusiasm. I am very glad of that. I think it is an excellent thing for all concerned. But you will remember, won't you, that if I fail to see the light and run afoul, in my writings, of the New Dispensation, it will not be because of love for Mencken or for any ulterior motives but because I have an honest conviction to express? There ought to be some interesting battles and when the smoke clears away—well, we will have had the excitement anyhow.[40]

Rascoe wrote at least three articles ridiculing the New Humanists. The first of these was his review in *Plain Talk* of the New Humanists' symposium, *Humanism in America,* edited by Norman Foerster, in which he concluded that the New Humanists had no body of literature; that the essays by Paul Elmer More, T. S. Eliot, Frank Jewett Mather, and Gorham Munson, among others, were based on ignorance and confusion; and that their leader, Irving Babbitt, was basically fascistic and was interested only in selling his books and in dialectics.[41] When Edgar Lee Masters read this article, he wrote to Rascoe that "Your article in *Plain Talk* on this thing called Humanism is a roaring piece of work, swift, energetic and hits hard. I am more than glad that you did it. Further it was a delight to see how you caught up Babbitt on Dante." The New Humanists were "deceivers and sophisters," "pedants," and "empty dialecticians," Masters said; and he hoped that Rascoe would "go on to annihilate their literary existence."[42]

In another of these articles, written for the Sunday magazine section of the *New York World,* Rascoe wrote what he considered to be an epitaph for the movement.[43] In this article he argued that "The present lure of this so-called humanism lies in its snob appeal to some young Americans whose literary equipment is complete, save for mental curiosity about life and the new and complex realities of chemistry, machinery, economics, psychology, and their effects upon man's thoughts, emotions and behavior." The New Humanists were the "intellectual nouveau riche," he said, "an hundred times more tory than tories bred and born."[44]

A third article attacking the New Humanists was Rascoe's contribution to *The Critique of Humanism,* a symposium which C. Hartley Grattan edited as a counterstatement to *Humanism in America.* Rascoe's contribution to this *Critique,* "Pupils of Polonius," was another attempt to make the New Humanists look foolish. Throughout Rascoe's essay, which included most of the material that had appeared in his *New York World* article, was this running piece of heavy irony: "It is not decorous; it is not moderation; it is not common sense for Professor Babbitt to. . . ." Rascoe's method of attack was to oversimplify the basic tenets of New Humanism so as to make its adherents—Babbitt, More, Eliot, J. Middleton Murry, and S. P. Sherman—look ridiculous. He praised Eliot's early work, but said that Eliot had now established "a rapprochement with his old Harvard teacher, Irving Babbitt," who was "the nearest thing to our Anglo-Catholic royalist in America."

And Babbit's ideas, Rascoe contended, "are simply those of a Boston Brahmin, holding a university chair, living in academic seclusion from contact with the world today, happily engaged, like a medieval schoolman, in shadowboxing with the ghost of Jean-Jacques Rousseau, who epitomizes to Professor Babbitt all of the anarchic, destructive and mistaken sentiments of man." Furthermore, Rascoe concluded, this Polonius "doesn't know how literature is created" and, in fact, "has a positive distaste for literature. . . ."[45] O. W. Firkins, in reviewing *The Critique of Humanism* in *The Saturday Review of Literature*, singled out the effectiveness of Rascoe's satire, saying that "he implants in the reader, like Poe or Maeterlinck, a new shudder—almost a disdain."[46]

VIII *Rascoe's Work Attacked by Ezra Pound*

In 1932, in a literary argument in the *New York Sun*, Rascoe and Ezra Pound resumed hostilities—this time about Rascoe's work. Pound, in a letter to the *Sun*, said that Rascoe only wrote about "established" authors, and that Rascoe had lied (in an earlier column in the *Sun*)[47] when he had said that he had written about Hemingway's "early experiments in the Transatlantic Review."[48] Rascoe replied in a letter to the *Sun* in which he gave the dates of his early articles on and reviews of Hemingway's work, of Eliot's, and of Pound's, among others. Perhaps Pound "had better just go down and give himself up," Rascoe wrote. "His greatest contribution to political science has been his hysterical advocacy of Mussolini and Fascism, not only for Italy but for the world." He then reminded Pound that, in a review of Eliot's *Poems* in the *Chicago Tribune* in 1920, he had pointed out Eliot's indebtedness to Corbière, "an influence not noted by others until some five years later," that he had written about Rémy de Gourmont "two years before Pound began to write about him in the Little Review" (in 1918, long after Gourmont's death), and that he had written about Proust's *Du Côté de chez Swann* in the *Chicago Tribune* in 1918 while Proust was still alive. Rascoe also reminded Pound that he had written an article about him in the *Chicago Tribune* in 1917 entitled "Let's Put

Ezra in the Pound," which began: "Slowly evidence is piling up to corroborate my early expressed estimate of Ezra Pound as a literary fourflusher of the most obnoxious kind."⁴⁹

Though Pound was wrong in his facts, his attack did herald the critical reaction to Rascoe's work that was imminent. *Titans* was well received later that year—in fact, the best received of all of Rascoe's books; but it clearly marked the apogee of his writing career; after *Titans* a gradual decline in his powers as editor and critic began. Yet, in reviewing Rascoe's *We Were Interrupted* in 1947, Maxwell Geismar praised Rascoe's work in these formative and decisive years (for Rascoe and for American literature); and he commented on some of the examples of Rascoe's work that we have already discussed. After stating his belief that Rascoe was a central figure in the literary movement that began in Chicago, Geismar added: "During Rascoe's editorship of The New York Tribune book pages, the period when he wrote 'A Bookman's Daybook,' one notices again his vitality and imagination as an innovator. The estimate of the 'Algonquin group' is very shrewd, the campaign against the 'Humanists' is almost as vivid now as it was in that golden day when literary feuds vied with oil scandals in the columns of the daily press." Geismar then concluded: "In the tradition of Huneker and H. L. Mencken himself, Rascoe was, in the middle Twenties, one of those who seemed to be raising our literary journalism to the level it occupies in France or England."⁵⁰

CHAPTER *4*

Reputation and Critical Reception

I *Teens: Chicago*

R ASCOE WAS remarkably successful as a literary editor and
critic in the late World War I period in Chicago. His book
pages in the *Chicago Tribune* were known in Paris, Dublin, London, New York, Boston, Baltimore, and Philadelphia, as shown
by quotations from his pages in the *Mercure de France;* the
London Mercury; Franklin P. Adams' column, "The Conning
Tower," in the *New York Tribune;* and in Mencken's column in
the *Sun.* In May, 1918, Mencken in the *Baltimore Evening Sun*
declared Chicago to be the "literary capital of the United States,"
pointing out that "For six months there has been a war over him
(Cabell) in Chicago, the town of pioneers in all the arts. Out
there Burton Rascoe (another fellow to be heard of later on)
whoops and declaims for him with the utmost ferocity."[1]

Rascoe's part in this literary war in Chicago was later recalled
by Harry Hansen who wrote that, "When I got back from the
Peace Conference and started the ... reviewing of books[,]
Chicago was having a literary renaissance and authors were
popping all over the place. ... on Saturdays the intelligentsia
would rush the newsstands for the Chicago 'Tribune' to find out
what Burton Rascoe was saying about H. L. Mencken, Marcel
Proust, George Jean Nathan, Dante, James Huneker, Dreiser and
an unknown and somewhat devious stylist named James Branch
Cabell."[2]

According to Maxwell Geismar, Rascoe was such a central figure in the literary movement in Chicago that "At times indeed,
such was the sense of literary excitement, the aura of discoveries
and triumphs that he radiated, [that] he seemed to be the movement."[3] Edmund Wilson has also commented on the distinctive
qualities of Rascoe's work: "In Chicago, he has performed the
astonishing feat of making literature exciting to the readers of a

great western paper. . . . At that distance, he has been obliged to develop senses preternaturally keen for perceiving signs of intellectual activity—and he has become almost telepathically aware— at a time when comparatively few people were aware of them— of Mencken in Baltimore, of Hergesheimer in Philadelphia, of Cabell in Richmond, of Conrad Aiken in Boston, of almost everybody, in fact, everywhere." Wilson then compared Rascoe to Mencken: "Perhaps no other American critic at that time, with the exception of Mencken himself, had so prompt and comprehensive an intelligence of what was being written in the United States."[4]

Conrad Aiken in Boston wrote to Rascoe about his editorial achievement on the *Chicago Tribune*, "You certainly run the best litry page in the country, no joking. Why don't you get the job of editing the Bookman or something of that sort?"[5] And Lewis Galantière also wrote to Rascoe about Rascoe's "Saturday Page": "I'd rather do it [book reviewing] for your page (aside from our friendship) than any other I've seen. It sparkles, it challenges, it provokes, it informs, it entertains: it is the best damned page of Lit stuff in the country. . . ."[6] Dreiser wrote to ask Rascoe to send him "25 copies of just your page—not the whole paper with a bill." He said that "Mr. Mencken has but now sent me a copy of your review of 'Twelve Men.' It is so understanding and so forceful that I am moved to send copies to friends here and there."[7]

In New York, Alfred A. Knopf wrote to Rascoe in 1919 about a series of French translations he planned to publish, for which Rascoe had agreed to write the introductions, and noted: "You are a really bookish person, so send me any ideas you have as to the physicial appearance of the books also."[8] And Hugh Walpole told Rascoe in a letter in 1920, "I am writing because I suggested your name to [Sir John Collings] Squire of the 'London Mercury' as the best possible writer of an American letter for that paper."[9]

Numerous others followed Rascoe's career in Chicago and have written about it. Vincent Starrett, as one example of many, wrote that, "As a literary editor of the Chicago *Tribune*, Burton made an astonishing reputation in a very short time. He cheered for Anatole France, and Rémy de Gourment [*sic*], and James Branch Cabell and Sherwood Anderson and Conrad Aiken and Joseph Hergesheimer, and a dozen or two more of whom Chicago, as a

reading whole, knew little enough beyond their names. He conducted sizzling rows with his critical contemporaries on the other
journals, suavely insulted the most popular writers of the day so
that they wrote furious replies, which he printed with delight,
and generally pepped up the culture of the community."[10] Starrett
stressed Rascoe's abilities as a controversialist: "He contradicted
the Great God Mencken, and arranged an exchange of incivilities
between Cabell and Rupert Hughes that must take its place be-
side the Whistler-Ruskin controversy. In short, he raised a great
deal of hell in Chicago, and his influence is still felt."

II *New York: 1920's*

Shortly after Rascoe went to work for *McCall's* in New York in
1921, Lewis Galantière wrote to him, evaluating Rascoe as a literary critic and advising him in his work; Galantière told Rascoe
that "... you do not need to feel yourself in competition with
critics in America, including Boyd, Mencken and Brooks or any
of the others. You have it over them like a tent, and you may
write slowly and publish rarely without thinking that you are
losing time or falling behind the parade." He then compared
Rascoe to Boyd, Mencken, and Brooks: "Mencken is a roaring,
sentimental bourgeois in the manner of Hercules; Boyd employs
in his criticism platitudes of general journalistic reviews which
even I should be ashamed to use; Brooks has a fine sensibility
and is a good student but his mind is static, he lacks curiosity,
fire and bowels. Go slowly, and reflect a little more before writing." And he said of Rascoe: "... you have both a wide, superficial knowledge, but very wide, arising out of an insatiable intellectual curiosity and a deep acquaintance with, and fine feeling
for literature and for the beautiful in general."[11]

From Galantière's letter, we can infer that Rascoe had expressed regrets about taking the *McCall's* job, fearing that it
might be the end of his career as a critic. We know that he had
written the day before to Cabell that "I have a good meal-ticket
at the above address."[12] The "above address" was the *McCall's*
letterhead, and the word "meal-ticket" suggests his feeling about
the job.

Both in Chicago and New York Rascoe was repeatedly asked
to collect his newspaper articles to make books. Cabell's request

on November 22, 1919, was typical: "To come to the real gist of this note, though, I do most earnestly want you to make a book of your newspaper articles. I know of few things that I desire more. . . . I thought of you and gnashed me teeth as I read [Mencken's] *Prejudices*: here was a fine and delightful book made up of material of which you were keeping a vastly superior brand interned [*sic*] in your scrapbook." Galantière was still entreating Rascoe to do this in the mid-1920's: "You certainly will have to get out a book. There are no two ways about that. I recognize that the difficulty is that you, who have some self-respect, hesitate to make up a book in the way others do, and I honor you for it. But you must do something about it. The Day-book had stuff enough of value to make a big volume."[13]

After Rascoe had become literary editor of the *New York Tribune* in 1922, Frank Moore Colby wrote to tell him that "It was a great pleasure to write for you when you were on the [Chicago] 'Tribune' for I liked very much the spirit of your own text and found great comfort in your liberal point of view."[14] F. Scott Fitzgerald also wrote, saying "You have certainly done wonders with the pages in the [New York] Tribune."[15] And Malcolm Cowley, writing from France, remarked on the editorial changes that Rascoe had made on the *Tribune*: "From time to time, even in Europe, I see a copy of the Sunday 'Tribune,' and I always turn to the book section first. You have done wonders with it. . . . In the old days . . . everything was vastly haphazard. Now it is a magazine for which one can write intelligently."[16]

In 1924 Rascoe became the subject of an essay by Isabel Patterson (Rascoe's assistant on the *New York Tribune*) in *The Literary Spotlight,* a book made of thirty anonymous portraits of leading literary figures in America at that time. Miss Patterson in her portrait wrote about Rascoe's great journalistic abilities:

> As a critic, he is a wonderful newspaper man. If he goes down in history at all, it will be as the encourager of new talents. He smells them out not by their artistic fragrance, but by virtue of as a keen a nose for news as ever any one was gifted with. His flair for the author who is going to write something startling is down-right uncanny. No one else in the world could have anticipated "Jurgen" by reading "The Cream of the Jest." One is already a classic; the other is just a *jeu d'esprit*. The men who have arrived don't interest Rascoe very much. You can learn all about them in

the morgue. What he is looking for is some one who will make fresh copy for tomorrow's paper. If he can get a novel angle on an established author, this is worthwhile; but otherwise, what's the use? Always there must be the perpetual slight novelty, with a timely application. . . .

. . . .

The original quality of the Daybook is that it reports the intellectual news of the day; here is the newspaperman to the fore, though he happens to be "covering" literature. The superficial gossip is mere window dressing. Mr. Rascoe is intent primarily upon giving a reflection of contemporary thought. And he goes after it like a reporter; gets it from the source.[17]

While in Paris in the fall and winter of 1924, Rascoe had been interviewed by Victor Llona for *Le Journal Littéraire*, and Llona's article on Rascoe became the source of a literary argument that developed in the *Chicago Tribune*. The pros and cons of Rascoe's literary judgments in Llona's article, entitled "La Littérature française jugée par les grands écrivains étrangers,"[18] were argued in Eugene Jolas' column, "Literary Paris," in the *Chicago Tribune* on February 22 and March 1, 1925. Llona himself defended Rascoe's competence in a letter in Jolas' column:

In interviewing Burton Rascoe, the point I had to consider was primarily whether my interlocutor was or was not qualified to voice worthwhile opinions about the literature of France. The questions I put to him and the answers he made to them were exclusively concerned with that particular subject. American writers were mentioned only in so far as they were thought to be influenced by French masters. It happened that I never met Burton Rascoe in America, but I had read many of his articles, from which I gathered the impression that he was very much *au courant* of French literature. I found in him a man who evidently knew the work of French writers better than by hearsay and who voiced opinions which could not fail to convey a certain amount of illuminating information to French readers. Unfortunately for lack of space all that he told me could not find its way into Le Journal Littéraire.[19]

Lewis Galantière, in a letter in Jolas' column, also defended Rascoe's "Day Book" against a correspondent's attack, pointing out that "It was common, at one time, to depreciate 'The Daybook.' " But, Galantière said, "When, as he shortly will, Rascoe publishes extracts from his rubric in book form, there will be what is called in America (and this time quite properly) a re-action in favor of 'The Daybook.'" This letter-writing argument itself, Galantière argued, "amply proves my main contention, which is that Rascoe made literature a subject of lively interest to many Americans."[20]

Rascoe's first book, *Theodore Dreiser*, published in 1925, drew congratulatory letters from Galantière and Dreiser. Galantière, on August 5, 1925, wrote that it "is an enchanting book, full of vigor and sense and persuasion, written from exactly the right point of view and hitting just the people who most want smashing. The old boy ought to be tickled to pieces. He emerges a lovable man, a great writer, and a human being of great and simple dignity. I can't tell you how pleased I am with the quality and brilliance of the book. ... your first book is great. ..." Dreiser was "tickled." He had already written Rascoe, on July 17, 1925, saying that "I love the beauty and incisiveness of your mind and the keen and kindly way in which you have interpreted me. An excellent and forceful piece of writing. Your shewing [*sic*] up of my idiosyncrasies and weaknesses makes me laugh—the rest—well, see above."

III A Bookman's Daybook

Rascoe's second book, *A Bookman's Daybook,* was a book made up of selections from his "Day Book," and was edited in 1929 by C. Hartley Grattan. In the Introduction Grattan wrote that "Burton Rascoe has always appealed to me, so long as I have been literarily conscious, as one of the truly worthwhile critics of the day. ... He seems more responsive to the significant literary currents of the time than any other single man whose vocation is literature. ..."[21] To Grattan, Rascoe was "the epitome of the New York literary spirit. ... It is almost possible to make a trip around the cultural world in Rascoe's writings."[22]

Edmund Wilson said in *The New Republic* in his review of Rascoe's *Daybook* that "He brings to it all his shrewdness, his audacity, his humor, his extraordinary memory and his undiscourageable enthusiasm for literature."[23] The reviewer for *The Nation* wrote that "This volume must take its place among the valuable records of twentieth century American literature and life."[24] And Henry Hazlitt, in a group review of Eliot's *Lancelot Andrews: Essays on Style and Order,* Herbert Read's *English Prose Style,* Julian Benda's *Belphegor,* and Rascoe's *Daybook,* found the aliveness of Rascoe's criticism to be second only to Mencken's:

> To me the first quality of Rascoe as a critic is his intense alive-ness. In the criticism of academic writers like Babbitt and More, for all their learning, discrimination, urbanity, restraint, there is something comparatively dead and inert. Rascoe, whatever his shortcomings, is brilliantly and vibrantly alive. This sense of life comes partly, I think, from his rapid and vigorous style, and even more from his remarkable hospitality toward every sort of new talent. It is true that this hospitality often leads him astray. It is true that his "discoveries" are too often seen at four times life size. It is true that he unearths too many geniuses:
> Sherwood Anderson . . . is one of our indubitable geniuses.
> I think that Cabell's "Jurgen" is one of the indubitable master-pieces of literature. I think that "Paradise Lost" is not.
> . . . .
>
> And so on. Also he is sometimes in too much of a hurry to verify his minor facts.
> But these slips may easily be forgiven; they are lost in the general gusto. Whatever the occasional errancies of his judgment, Rascoe is no mere literary gossip; his discussions of Eliot and Anatole France, for example, are shrewd and highly discriminat-ing pieces of criticism, and everything he sets down has amazing readability. In brief, with the sole exception of Mencken, he has done more than any other living American critic to make literature seem *exciting*.[25]

Finally, William Rose Benét wrote in *The Bookman* that he thought that Rascoe's

> running comment on American writing and writers of his time is one of the best things of its kind that have ever appeared in a newspaper. Look the others over who are doing it now—and then go back to this book. It isn't merely that there is no stereotype in it; there is intelligence, there is intimacy of the mind, there is vitality and high spirits—even—when he girds at one whom I consider the star among comrades, Christopher Morley. . . . there are few able diarists in America. Rascoe turns out to be one

who can be culled from and preserved with the hope of some
permanence. He had the ear for the illuminating anecdote.

When he picked winners he picked winners; which isn't, after
all, so easy as it may seem. He knew the worth of many authors
before the fanfare began. And a thing that one likes about the man
in this book of his is his human independence. He was frank and
honest about his predilections and his prejudices. He observed
everybody from his own particular corner, and he was the only
one in it.[26]

Malcolm Cowley, after arguing with Rascoe about the merits
of the selection he had made from the *Daybook* to use in *Exile's
Return*, wrote in a letter to the *New York Herald Tribune* what
he thought about the *Daybook*. He said, "It's a strikingly honest
attempt to set down what a literary editor read, thought and
heard in the years 1922–24. It's full of low buffoonery, gossip . . .
and downright silliness, but all this is considerably mixed with
observation, learning and first-rate criticism. Rascoe didn't try to
edit himself; he set down his day-by-day impressions, good, bad,
wise, stupid, with complete and engaging candor. That is what
makes this book a valuable and entertaining record."[27] Rascoe
had argued that Cowley had selected a piece of "low buffoonery"
from the *Daybook* and had made it seem representative of the
quality and content of the book.

IV Titans of Literature: *1930's*

On November 1, 1932, Rascoe's longest book, *Titans of Literature: From Homer to the Present,* was published. Carl Van Doren
had read some of the chapters of the manuscript before publication, and had written this comment on them to Rascoe: "God
what fun your chapters have given me! I see I was right. This was
just the sort of book that was needed, and you were just the man
to write it. I've laughed and exulted my way through every line
you let me see. Exulted at seeing all those heads swatted.
Laughed at seeing all those bottoms spanked. And besides these
lively pleasures I've had no end of intense satisfaction at seeing
how often you have put your sympathetic finger on true merits
and made it clear how much they deserve your generous acute
tributes. It's a very learned book, too. Lively learning—the most
pleasant thing a book can have. I'm really delighted with it,
and proud to have been allowed to see the manuscript."[28] Lane

Cooper, professor at Cornell University, had read the chapters of the manuscript on the Greek writers; and he had written to Rascoe that "Your treatment of the Greek writers is fresh and independent. It has made me reconsider some of my own judgments."[29]

On the day of publication William Soskin, in his column in the *New York Evening Post*, recalled his first acquaintance with Rascoe's criticism and what it had meant to him. "When I met Burton Rascoe in the columns of the Bookman's Day Book of the New York 'Tribune' almost a decade ago," he said, "I experienced a rekindling of some of the excitement about books which had almost been crowded out of my system by a thorough course in academic consumption of literature.... In Burton Rascoe's critical discussions there was an excitement, a sense of living news, an authority that gave me confidence once more in my own humble processes of human thinking." Soskin advised that *Titans* "must not be regarded as a blatant piece of debunking; [it does] destroy scholastic myths and talmudic distortions, [but] out of an essential love for the greater things contained in the original matter....'Titans'... confirms my faith in the fundamental health of Rascoe's criticism. It has the natural, spontaneous, honest emphasis of the free man in a world made dull by polite, timid and dim-witted professors. And it is founded in genuine learning."[30]

On the same day Lewis Gannett said in his column in the *Herald Tribune* that he believed that, "If some wide-awake professor, ignoring the unimportant factual errors with which 'Titans of Literature' is studded, should adopt this volume as a textbook, he will be astonished to discover how eagerly college boys can read the classics." Gannett prophesied, however, that "There will be stuffy professors to protest against Rascoe's mistakes and irreverences; but only those who, obsessed with midget facts, are blind to the great fresh, contagious reverence with which Rascoe proclaims the glories of the great men whom he has rediscovered. This is post-Stracheyan writing; it was necessary to 'debunk' before great men could be appreciated in their simple, humble greatness."[31]

Later, commenting on *Titans* in his column in *Scribner's Magazine*, William Lyon Phelps fulfilled Gannett's prophecy. He began his protest with "It is seldom I have read a worse book in literary criticism than *Titans*...." Phelps even objected to the book's being published: "This was written by request, and the requester did [Rascoe] a sharp disservice. It is a pity, for the author is an accomplished journalist and columnist, and must be a most agreeable person, in fact a 'jolly good fellow.'. . . If the chapters in this large volume had been prepared for reading aloud to some small group of intimates, well and good; but why print them? . . . It is the brashness, the genial vulgarity, the good-natured, cheerful barging into holy ground, that becomes so trying. . . ."[32]

The *New York Times* reviewer, J. Donald Adams, offered a sounder, more detailed analysis. He said of *Titans*:

> The current season offers no livelier reading, either for those whose primary interest is literature or for those who can take books or leave them alone. Had it been published in the years when five dollars (which would then have been its price) was not a stake against adversity but merely a bill of the smaller denominations, it would conceivably have had a sale comparable to that of "The Story of Philosophy.". . .
>
> [Rascoe] writes with a verve and gusto, with a skilled command of both bludgeon and rapier . . . which are altogether his own.
>
> Mr. Rascoe's approach to his subject is as fresh as the viewpoint of those Greeks with whom he opens his survey. . . . There is good common sense in his insistence that we bear in mind concerning the Greeks of the classic age that they were, after all, people and not chiseled embodiments of the good, the true, and the beautiful. There are no better chapters in his book than those which he devotes to Homer, Hesiod and the Greek dramatists. . . .[33]

Adams, who half-agreed with Rascoe's unorthodox views on Dante and Milton, added that "Rascoe's analysis of Milton the man is one of his best biographical performances, although all the biographical sections in his book are admirably done." And he argued successfully that Rascoe's "preference is strongly for prose as a medium of expression, and that while not insensitive to poetry, his feeling for it is much less sure and much less deeply felt." He presented an abundance of evidence to support this: that the qualities Rascoe admired in poetry were the qualities more properly belonging to prose; that Rascoe treated poets almost entirely biographically, except Dante and Milton; that Rascoe was fond of Latin poets, whose kinship with prose writers is closer than usual; that he wrote of wit in Villon's poetry, of verbal music in Verlaine's; and that "Mr. Rascoe's deepest enthusiasms are for wit and satire, for the revelation of human character, for the qualities which are soonest found in the great prose writers, not for the more tenuous properties of the poets." Thus, Adams concluded, Rascoe's chapters on the prose writers are "of greater value than his chapters on the poets. They are splendidly done, both as to the lives of these men and as to the nature of their contributions to the world's literature."[34]

In a letter Murray Godwin told Rascoe that "'Titans' is the most stimulating, keenest, most genuinely informative thing [I] have ever read on Homer and the Greeks, Virgil and the Romans, Dante and the Middle Ages. . . . All told a splendid job. . . . We love your unclouded faculty for seeing the most worn and conventionalized phenomena as new and different and fresh, as in Homer and the Homeridae, Sophocles and his prodigious lack of high ethical struggle." And, he added, "The passages dealing with Greek pronounciation are not only, I believe, great scholarship but great prose art. They are quiet, thoughtful, firm, and sure, and together they carry, communicate conviction without a trace of violence. . . ."[35] Godwin later reviewed *Titans* in *The New Republic,* commenting there that "There is something in [Rascoe's] eye and approach that lets him see even the most taken-for-granted cultural images in aspects invisible to those whom scholarship has submerged." He added that "a good share of [Rascoe's work] has been keen, highly original, penetratingly acute— nourishment of the best. . . ." Godwin said that he had found in *Titans* "an overtone of enthusiasm almost electrical in its intensity and in its communicability. . . ."[36]

In a long review, Alan Burton Clarke judged Rascoe's book accurately. Clarke found *Titans* "absorbingly interesting," and recommended it to "all mature students of world literature." Like many other reviewers, he found the book's chief virtue to be its "gusto"; "after one recovers from the destructive blasts in the opening chapters, the book moves forward on the sheer enthusiasm of its author." The book was not a history of literature, he noted, though there was history in it, and a great deal of "sound, revealing criticism"; rather, it was "chiefly a record of a writer with wide sympathies and strong convictions about what he likes and, to some degree, why [he] likes it."

Clarke then praised Rascoe's chapters on the Greek and Latin literatures for being free of pedantry, even though they were "wildly eccentric"; and he said of Rascoe's chapters on Rabelais and Proust that they "can excite little else than unreserved commendation." He also liked Rascoe's "wise and gentle treatment" of Mark Twain, which he said was "something positively unique in contemporary criticism." In conclusion, he said that he doubted the value of *Titans* as reasoned criticism; but, "for flashes of insight and warmth of feeling and interpretation, it is a constant delight." He recommended that the book be required reading in American colleges, adding that he had once been a college professor and that he knew what good it would do.[37]

Professor Robert S. Illingworth, of Clarke University, Worcester, Massachusetts, did use *Titans* as a text in his course Appreciation of Literature. In a letter to G. P. Putnam's Sons, publishers of *Titans*, dated March 1, 1933, Professor Illingworth said: "After careful reading of the book, it seemed to me that it would be more stimulating to students than any other book that I have found in this field."

C. Hartley Grattan, reviewing *Titans* for *Scribner's Magazine,* wrote that he believed that Rascoe was

probably the last of the literary journalists who actually reads Greek and Latin for pleasure and who is capable of writing an excursus on the translation and pronounciation of classical Greek. His unusual equipment has allowed him to examine most of his material in the original languages and by concentrating on texts rather than commentaries, he has found out for himself whether the works are to be pronounced living or dead.

Bringing his lively intelligence to bear upon them, he has discovered wherein they are human and just when and in what words they still have something to say to us. Fortunately Rascoe is not entirely literary. Though he protesteth much against the social interpretation of literature (which he does not quite understand) he nevertheless is aware in his own way that literature is continuous with life and that literary values are, after all, life values expressed after a certain fashion. His writers always live and move in a visible world, for he tells you plainly what the world was like when they were alive.

The chapters devoted to the Greek writers are especially to be recommended as full of sense and vigor. Rascoe has had the courage to assign to the Roman writers a low value in general, though he distinguishes those who did manage to say something worthwhile.

Rascoe brings to literature a vigorous, devouring interest which he communicates to the reader in a vivid and compelling prose. Whether it be Homer or tomorrow's novel, Rascoe's discussion is, in the best sense, news. In this book he brings his peculiar qualities to their apogee.[38]

But in December *The Saturday Review of Literature* published letters headed "This Will Never Do" by Edith Hamilton and Donald A. Roberts strongly attacking Rascoe's *Titans*. Miss Hamilton said satirically of Rascoe, "He has stormed the ancient, undemocratic, privileged citadel of the scholar and the critic and has handed it over to democracy triumphant." Mr. Roberts attacked both Rascoe's book and the critics who praised it: ". . . it is ridiculous for a man to be called vivid, lively, enthusiastic, exciting, alert, honest, spontaneous and frank if he has no facts on which to base his judgment. . . . The columnists and journalists who pose as critics do not possess the knowledge or judgment necessary to fulfill their function. A man or woman who calls the substance of this book scholarship or literary criticism, or recommends it as 'just the sort of book that was needed' is either hopelessly or wilfully ignorant."[39]

Ernest Boyd in a review of *Titans* in *The Nation* preferred to view Rascoe as "a superb journalist" and *Titans* as an example of the lost art of literary journalism:

Mr. Rascoe, in this Great Republic of newspapermen, is that unique phenomenon, a literary journalist. He has, that is to say, as keen an interest in literature as the average newspaperman has in booze, baseball, and the platitudes of politicians; he can make literature as lively a news topic as the usual sport and political bilge which newspapers and their newspapermen delight to honor; and he can, at the same time, render real service to literature and its unfortunate victims.

When Mr. Rascoe edited the literary supplement of the *New York Tribune*, that overgrown village actually witnessed a first-rate literary journalist at work. Needless to say, that did not last very long. Mr. Rascoe failed to dish up the platitudes meant for all time as if they were the latest news. He was—apparently—a bad newspaperman. But he was a superb journalist.

In a sense, *Titans of Literature* is another *Outline of Philosophy*, save for the fact that Mr. Durant has never, I imagine, sent anybody to the original works of the writers of whom he speaks, whereas Mr. Rascoe's heresies and enthusiasms are designed to provoke an immediate response to the authors whom he discusses. For the accepted figures of world literature he does in this volume what he did editorially on the *Tribune* for the literature of the world.[40]

Of course, Boyd said, specialists could detect errors in a work so comprehensive in character as *Titans;* yet the book had "the charming vitality of Mr. Rascoe's interest in all literature, his obvious belief that great books are alive and of a thrilling interest, that they should not be left to the dead hands of the professors, whose delight it is to champion the great and the mediocre alike, provided they are dead." Boyd agreed with Rascoe's judgments on the Romans and the Greeks:

> In this connection Mr. Rascoe's onslaught on the Romans, the dreariest bores in recorded history, and their dreary literature should be read by all intelligent youngsters. As Mr. Rascoe insists, the greatest Latin writers are not the pets of the pedagogues— Cicero, Virgil, and those other horrors of schooldays—but Petronius, Horace, Catullus, and Propertius. . . . He rightly points out that Greek was the cultured language, and that if one must read an epic it is better to go to the Greek original than to the stilted Latin copy; that there is nothing anywhere in Latin comparable to Aristophanes, Thucydides, Aeschylus, Euripides, Sophocles, Herodotus; that even Xenophon was never so dull, despite his parasangs, as Caesar, with his ablative absolutes. . . .
> Even when his scholarship is unimpeachable, no pedant will approve, because he bases his likes and dislikes upon personal human emotions, and not upon the theory of what is and what is not the right thing.[41]

Finally, Archibald Henderson, perceiving both the good and bad in *Titans,* judged it on its intention, and found it

> . . . a fascinating and vexatious, devout yet reverent, studiously prepared yet antipedantic work, by a breezy, impudent idol smasher.
> There is not a dull page in the book. I have read every line of it, with zest and gusto; yet in many places with reservation and depreciation. Think of covering the field of world literature from Homer to Joyce, in the mood of H. L. Mencken—not the narrow and parochial H. L. M. we know, alas! so well, but a sophisticated

H. L. M. with considerable catholicity of taste, culture of no
mean order, and a bright engaging, journalistic style.

[*Titans*] is a strange mélange of impertinence, scorn and deri-
sion, frequently interspersed with delicate appreciation, warm
admiration, and acute criticism.

... the essays on Boccaccio, Villon, Dickens and France are
admirable; whereas those on Dante, Shakespeare, Milton and
Mark Twain are an almost total loss. Like all outline books the
primary interest is biographical; and here Rascoe shines, again
and again.

But far be it from me to complain! The book constantly in-
trigued and irked me. I finished it both *enchanté et bafoué*. What
more can we ask of a book conceived in this vein, and executed
in this manner?[42]

Though all of the reviewers noted its faults, almost all of them
praised *Titans* for its human qualities—for its energy, "gusto,"
"amazing vitality," aliveness, readability, and independent judgments. *Titans* marked the high point in Rascoe's career as a critic.
Paradoxically, however, it marked the beginning of his decline;
for, after *Titans*, the reaction to subjective criticism—which had
threatened to develop in the early 1920's—set in. Rascoe himself
ironically in his "Notes for an Epitaph: H. L. Mencken" had
clearly sounded the signal. So for Rascoe, with the publication of
Titans in 1932, the era of criticism that had begun during World
War I was over, and a new one had begun. New criteria for
judging art were in the ascendancy, which Rascoe futilely tried
to combat. He continued to maintain his critical standards and
techniques in the face of the Marxist-oriented critics of art, the
psychological critics, and the New Critics. But he could never
again regain the hold on the reading public's imagination that he
once had. This decline was gradual, of course, and at least
through the 1930's he was still able to command an audience
appreciative enough of his style and views, and large enough, to
assure him of getting writing jobs. Increasingly, however, it
became harder and harder for him to find outlets for what he
had to say.

V Prometheans

Rascoe's *Titans* was followed by *Prometheans, Ancient and
Modern;* and on December 1, 1933, the first reviews of *Prome-*

theans appeared. Though most of the reviewers still praised Rascoe's style, the consensus was that *Prometheans* was inferior to *Titans,* and that only parts of the book were any good. Bruce Catton, writing for the Newspaper Enterprise Association Service, accurately called *Prometheans* a "potboiler," saying that it "lacks the solidity of its predecessor." Catton did like parts of the book, however, as did most of the reviewers.[43] Howard Mumford Jones in *The Saturday Review of Literature* called *Prometheans* "a good idea imperfectly executed." Jones did not like Rascoe's selection of Prometheans; and he thought the essays were "uncertain," pointing out that "Nietzsche . . . is discussed in less than nine pages—a thoroughly unsatisfactory performance from a critic of Mr. Rascoe's reputation."[44]

Many of the critics and reviewers compared and contrasted *Titans* and *Prometheans,* and *Prometheans* always fared badly. The reviewer of *Prometheans* for the *Philadelphia Public Ledger* said that "Had Burton Rascoe's 'Prometheans' preceded his 'Titans of Literature,' no doubt it would have stood up well on its own merits. Instead, it follows that remarkable volume of wit, wisdom, assault and acidulous criticism, and it suffers by comparison. The first thought is that it is a gathering of left-over material from Rascoe's earlier book; but more likely it is merely left-over opinion. . . ."[45] Fannie Butcher, in the *Chicago Tribune,* commented that " 'Prometheans,' following that intriguing and stimulating 'Titans'. . . is a disappointment, since it has neither the consistency of form nor of matter which its predecessor had."[46]

Sculley Bradley's evaluation of *Prometheans* in the *Philadelphia Record* was a typical one; he pointed out, as did many others, that *Prometheans* was a "provocative, interesting and valuable book. But not as good as *Titans*." Its chief value, like that of *Titans,* was its success "in making literature a living subject. . . ." But Bradley did not think that Rascoe had always selected true Prometheans to write about: "It seems clear that five of the nine authors bore no Promethean fire, although some of them had sooty hands; and Mr. Cabell bears only a hollow reed. . . . Only two of the authors treated are clearly Prometheans —Saint Mark and Friedrich Nietzsche." Bradley did not believe that Cabell, Dreiser, Aretino, Petronious, nor even Lucian were true Prometheans: they were not marked by a "willing acceptance of suffering in the service of a great and life-shaking idea."

Yet, considered by other standards, some of the essays were excellent, Bradley noted. "The best is the treatment of Lucian, one
of the finest essays on a classical writer ever written for the
inspiration of a modern and ignorant generation." "Thus," Bradley concluded, "there is much to recommend this book."[47]

After Dreiser had read Rascoe's *Prometheans* in 1934, he immediately got off a letter to Rascoe in which he expressed his
opinion of the book:

> I have finished "Prometheans" practically at one sitting. All in
> all, I think very highly of it, and for the following reasons: In the
> first place whatever the sources of your material, the treatment
> of it is so modern and engagingly intimate, that I found it delight-
> ful. So much so, that I wish it were possible for you to re-survey
> a great deal of history in just this way. You eliminate all the
> tedium that goes with stilted, or shall I say carefully phrased
> scholasticism. Of all the papers in the book, I'm sure I like "St.
> Mark" the best. The style is, as I say, and the material immensely
> illuminating to me. At last I have an intelligent line on the origins
> of Christianity, and I am grateful for that. The next best paper to
> me is "Lucian," with its picture of the Roman world of his day.
> And after that, I think I like "Petronius," and "Apuleius," and
> then "Aretino." Personally, I feel that you are a little short of an
> adequate grasp of D. H. Lawrence's solar plexis theory. . . .
>
> I think the study of myself is excellent and sound, but some of
> your data is a little off. [Dreiser corrects Rascoe on a few minor
> points of fact.][48]

In the rest of the letter, Dreiser suggested that Rascoe was "a
little too indifferent to your own very great ability. For a person
who can do a piece of work like 'St. Mark' can do a lot of very
important things." He told Rascoe that "I know from reading
this book of yours that now you are mentally equipped to make
a brilliant success of [re-establishing *The Bookman*],[49] or anything of that kind."

VI *Rascoe Attacked and Defended*

But by the mid-1930's the countermovement implicit in the
letters attacking *Titans* by Edith Hamilton and Donald A. Roberts
reasserted itself. In an article called "On 'Bad Boy' Criticism" in
The North American Review, L. B. Hessler attacked Rascoe and
his method of criticism. After quoting from Rascoe's essay on

"Milton" in *Titans*, which had been published three years earlier, Hessler wrote: "Now this is exactly what the bad boy does; he sticks out his tongue at his elders, he puts a banana skin where a dignified man with a silk hat will step on it. These ingratiating tricks, while pardonable in a small boy, are, in an adult, signs that he is not yet completely civilized; he is still a hick, a smart aleck. If one goes to Mr. Rascoe's book, *Titans of Literature*, for bread he will, for the most part, receive a stone; he will, to be sure, be amused—but the entertainment will not be great. Some of the essays are real exercises in criticism; others are prolonged statements of personal prejudices; still others are merely half-hearted biographical sketches."[50] Hessler denounced Rascoe's Classical learning and scholarship, as found in Rascoe's essay on Virgil and Latin literature in *Titans*, and disagreed with Rascoe's judgments on Dante and Milton; then he concluded that

> The expression of personal opinion is, of course, the right of everyone, but when it is done at the expense of accuracy and truth, the reader must enter a protest. There is a view today that criticism is but the expression of one's self, the adventures of a soul amongst masterpieces, that the critic is a creative artist of the same sort as a lyric poet. It is an interesting theory, but it depends for its validity on who the lyric adventurer is. Moreover, the critic has a responsibility toward the public that is not necessarily shared by the lyric poet; he assumes the manner of authority and must bear with him his credentials.
>
> The "bad boy" in criticism is obsessed with the notion that what is traditional is wrong, that what he dislikes everyone ought to dislike; and so he goes around sticking pins in the mighty. Judging from the violence of Mr. Rascoe's language in the essays on Sophocles, Virgil, Dante and Milton, one suspects that anything like religion and morality in an author is, to him, a major crime. There are, no doubt, certain aspects of goodness that are irritating to most honest persons; but to dismiss all literature that is, so to speak, tainted with morality, is to deprive oneself of a high form of pleasure, and, in a critic, it is a serious limitation.[51]

A similar attack appeared in *The Nation* two months later. According to the authors of this article, Margaret Marshall and Mary McCarthy, Rascoe was the leader of a group of anti-intellectual critics. Hershel Brickell and Isabel Patterson, they said, are "typical of one group of frontline critics, a group too amorphous to be called a school, as intensely personal as a social clique, a group whose most notable characteristic is its militant anti-intellectualism. At the head of this group is Burton Rascoe; its house organ is *Herald Tribune Books*, over which Irita Van Doren presides; its club is the Literary Guild."[52] Other members of this group, or people closely associated with it, were Carl Van Doren and Joseph Wood Krutch.[53]

This attack continued: "For this group literature must be 'exciting,' history and biography must read like fiction, and fiction must above all be entertaining and easy. Like the man on the street who rails against professors, this critical brotherhood pipes its complaint against the great men of letters. Unequipped to deal with complicated artistic or intellectual problems, they instinctively resist them and affect to despise them. They write rave notices of second-rate untaxing novels and send lists of the classics they have not read to *Books* and to *The Nation*. They plug their favorite writers, applaud one another's efforts, and bolster one another's opinions at literary teas." Using as evidence quotations from several of Rascoe's reviews, and quotations from *Titans*, the authors of this article concluded, first, that "Their pace-setter, Burton Rascoe, like William Lyon Phelps, deals in ready-made superlatives. We have already recorded his predilection for Thorton Wilder"; second, that "Mr. Rascoe is much concerned with 'humanizing' literature. In the course of performing his self-appointed task he sometimes finds it necessary to 'debunk' famous literary men . . ."; and, third, that "Mr. Rascoe remains influential. In the *Herald Tribune Books* he seldom rates anything less than the first page."[54]

Louis Paul, who read both this article in *The Nation* and Rascoe's column in *Esquire* that month, commented on both in a letter to Rascoe: "I enjoyed your review in Esquire. I wish desperately that there was more of this hot and personal questioning upon the part of our intellectual members of society. Missy Whoozis [Margaret Marshall] in the *Nation* accuses you of anti-intellectualism, whereas of course she is accusing herself of rigor mortis; her contention is that whatever one feels is traitorous; only ideas which embody the purity of complete divorce from reality are worth pronouncing. . . . The article was good. It was not too personal—this would be like saying Anatole France was a lousy writer because he was too human."[55]

One large part of Rascoe's work was that of writing introductions for books. In 1936, for example, he wrote the Introduction to The Limited Editions Club's *The Ballad of Reading Gaol,* and George Macy, director of the Club, wrote to congratulate Rascoe on this work: ". . . I think your introduction for *The Ballad of Reading Gaol* is among the best things you have written. . . . I didn't know that you were capable of so fine a survey of the Wildeian epoch. Your summary of the character of Oscar Wilde, your survey of his influence upon English literature, your animadversions upon the period of The Yellow Book, combine to make an introduction which should add considerable value to our edition."[56]

In 1937, Louis Paul wrote an article about Rascoe in which he said that "Sometimes I think [Rascoe] has succeeded where Ponce de Leon failed, and that he has somewhere a secret hoard of youth to which he returns. . . . The bane of book reviewer's trade is ennui. Books become cheap. Gissing hated literature with all the violence of a man poisoned with it, since he earned his living too long in Grub Street. . . . Burton Rascoe writes of books as though, out of enduring love, they had been bought with his last pennies."[57] In the rest of the article Paul discussed Rascoe's work and evaluated his importance:

> Unlike a hundred lesser scribblers possessed of a pompous self-importance, Rascoe has time for genuine friendship. He makes time, too, endlessly, for that highest of all philanthropy, the encouragement of new writers. I shan't soon forget my first meeting with him. He had read a story of mine, my first; and when he learned I had written novels I was unable to publish, invited me to his home for dinner. . . . There are literally hundreds [of potentially good writers] who weren't sure of it until Rascoe said so.
>
> . . . .
>
> A pioneer scholar to kick the dead stuffings out of literature, his critiques remain both lively and sound. His vitality and exuberance are sometimes called faults by sourpuss savants, who probably envy his erudition. . . .
>
> I don't know what makes good writing. . . . But I am beginning to suspect that the ability to convey a passionate excitement in it helps. If one can believe the current work of inexpressible importance to himself and the world in general it may have the

tendency to communicate this belief to the reader. Mr. Rascoe accomplishes this astonishing feat time after time.... With an undercurrent of sweet humor and in a style that is fluid as running water and as fluent as the automatic writing of a clairvoyant he brings to the least literary of readers a new conception and a new feeling for books. He can light up a subject that was born stuffy. Young, spirited, alive, interested, emotional, possessed of a warm and generous heart, he is fulfilling a function of tremendous importance.[58]

VII *Autobiography:* Before I Forget *and* We Were Interrupted

Before I Forget, published in May, 1937, was on best-seller lists, and most of its many reviewers praised it. *Time Magazine,* however, in a review sarcastically headed "Bright Boy," read bitterness by Rascoe into the book: "How his militant literary career soared so far is the explicit theme of *Before I Forget;* why it never rose far is the implicit question which between-the-line readers may be able to answer for themselves."[59] But John Chamberlain, reviewing *Before I Forget* in *The New Republic,* recognized Rascoe's contributions to America's literary awakening and defended him against such attacks. In his review, headed "Eye Opener," Chamberlain said that "Burton doesn't claim much for himself [in *Before I Forget*].... [He] is entirely too modest about his role as a literary journalist in a period when the United States stood in egregious need of the curiosity-cum-enthusiasm of literary journalists who loved the lusty in letters. The counts against Rascoe—that he overestimated people like Cabell and Hergesheimer, that he is sometimes inaccurate and occasionally downright unjust—do not seem to be very important.... Rascoe may not have been a systematic critic in the European tradition. But when men are blind they don't need systematic critics. They need eye-openers like Burton Rascoe."[60]

In a review of *Before I Forget* in *Harper's Magazine,* Harry Hansen put Rascoe's literary journalism—a "happy wedding of personality and idea"—in the European tradition and emphasized Rascoe's "amazing capacity for characterizing individuals, and for sketching the curious literary and journalistic events of the second decade of this century in Chicago." Hansen, who had worked in Chicago at that time, remembered that "Burton Rascoe's book reviews and columns of literary comment had nothing in common with the desiccated, formal, and conventional criticism practiced by his elders; he championed the writings of James Branch Cabell, H. L. Mencken, Theodore Dreiser, Conrad Aiken, and numerous other rebels against all comers...."[61]

We Were Interrupted was published in 1947, and the reviewers continued to praise Rascoe's contributions in the 1920's. For example, in a front-page laudatory review by Lloyd Morris in the *New York Herald Tribune*, Rascoe was pictured as having "spent most of the decade of the '20's at one or another outpost of critical warfare and revolutionary assault. He was a leader, as it were, at the barricades.... A varied series of editorial posts kept Rascoe at the vortex of literary activity."[62] Lewis Gannett, in the same newspaper, later minimized the importance of Rascoe's work, but added: "... there is no question that Mr. Rascoe had, and has, a talent for discovering the center of controversy and launching himself into it."[63] James Gray's review in *The Saturday Review of Literature* was typical of the reviews of *We Were Interrupted*. Gray noted:

> For [Rascoe] the times have been absolutely right. He is the essential twentieth-century American, and individualist who has been allowed to take the ruggedness of his enterprise into the field of letters and make an undisputed place for himself.
>
> Essentially he has been a man of books but his own philosophy that literature is about life has made him come romping down out of the ivory tower to engage in all the economic, social, and ideological feuds of the minute....
>
> The mood of the decade [portrayed in *We Were Interrupted*] which Rascoe perfectly shared was that of welcoming an entirely new age, one that was freer, bolder, more candid and critical than any America had known before.
>
> Rascoe believed fervently in that newness and wanted to give its audacity a good, clear, ringing voice in the special realm of criticism. ... he saw his task as being that of making literature exciting. The fact that he was very nearly always in the midst of a feud shows how well he succeeded.... If Rascoe's record as a literary critic were to be estimated in terms of the sober second thought that posterity is supposed to practice, it would be found to be good. In a great many instances reflective judgment has come to be in agreement with the opinion that he tossed off in the first flush of enthusiasm or of indignation. ... His intuitive recognition of a book's honest and vigorous impulses enables him to write out with a large sweeping hand sound judgments that he who can might read.

[Rascoe] points out, accurately, how many who have had
... cramping ideologies to defend have failed to be good critics.
A spinsterish concern with some special kind of correctness
would have killed the rugged receptivity of Rascoe's loves.[64]

We Were Interrupted was Rascoe's last work to get widespread
critical attention. And he has become since 1947 practically a
forgotten literary figure. Even his critical and editorial contributions to American literary life in the decade before and during
the 1920's have become obscured, dismissed, or distorted. He is
still mentioned in some of the literary histories and biographies
of literary figures of the period,[65] but none of his work is in print
today. Edmund Wilson summed it all up when he wrote, in a
sympathy note to Mrs. Rascoe shortly after Rascoe's death in
1957, that "He never gets full credit now for all he did in the
Twenties and before." Yet, Wilson pointed out, "In his best days
he was worth a dozen of the so-called New Critics."[66]

CHAPTER 5

Critical and Editorial Contributions

WILLIAM SOSKIN, in his review of *Before I Forget*, listed what he considered to be Rascoe's major contributions; he suggested that "Mr. Rascoe may prefer to be regarded as a great discoverer, a literary pioneer who beat the drum for Cabell and other heroes of the twenties, a rejuvenator of the classics, a discriminating and ironic critic—and he can claim all these positions with eminent justice. Most of us will appreciate him even more, however, for the refreshing human quality he brings to the all too professional world of authorship and publishing."[1] Soskin fails to list, however, what may be Rascoe's most important contribution—his work to help broaden, enlarge, and raise the level of American literature, a goal that inspired him in all of his critical battles.

I Champions a Distinctive American Literature

Rascoe's battles in the *Chicago Tribune*, for example, were an essential part of his lifelong plan to achieve this goal. For this reason, he spent so much time and energy vigorously ridiculing and attacking the ignorant English critics who frequently condemned all American writers and literature, and who attacked even the American language. In one of his articles he explained his attack on Edgar Jepson's views on American literature; Jepson, he said, had written a column in *The London Egoist* complaining that Rascoe (and Harriet Monroe) had abused him instead of "controverting his contention that all contemporary American poetry, except some lines by T. S. Eliot and Ezra Pound is . . . punk. . . ." Rascoe, admitting the abuse, said: "We did just that. . . . There is scarcely space in several complete issues of Poetry Magazine and The Tribune to educate an English writer of tenth-rate fiction in an appreciation of Masters, Frost, Aiken, Lindsay, Sandburg, et al. . . ." Jepson, Rascoe pointed out, ". . . doesn't even know that Mr. Frost's first name is Robert, not

Edgar ..."; yet he has displayed, Rascoe continued, "such colossal conceit as to condemn all modern American poetry ... on the strength of four isolated lines he does not like. ...The symptoms are those of paranoia than of critical insight."[2]

And in a review of John Drinkwater's play, *Abraham Lincoln,* which had been enthusiastically received in London, Rascoe told his readers that there was no need for Americans to feel that their contemporary literature was inferior. After showing how bad Drinkwater's play was in style and technique, Rascoe admonished Americans to have more pride in their own literature. Using soaring overstatement—a characteristic and favorite device of his in this kind of writing—he tried to persuade his readers to support American writers:

> Let us become a trifle self-conscious. We have proper pride in everything except in our literature, and in that we yield always with a servile acquiescence to Europe. At this moment it occurs to me that England (excluding Ireland) possesses no prose writers, excepting Hardy and Conrad, and possibly D. H. Lawrence, who have produced work comparable to that produced by the Americans James Branch Cabell, Theodore Dreiser, Henry K. Marks, Sherwood Anderson, and Joseph Hergesheimer. In poetry, of course, we lead the field over the contemporary entries not only from England but from France, and if you would gauge the difference between a conspicuous French novelist, say Barbusse, and a conspicuous American novelist, say Sherwood Anderson, compare the weak, mechanical 'We Others' with Anderson's impressive "Winesburg, O."[3]

To achieve his goal, Rascoe also wrote in 1918–19 a number of literary editorials designed to "foster the cause of good literature" and to combat America's "servile acquiescence to Europe." In one of these early editorials, headed "On a Certain Condescension in Our Natives,"[4] Rascoe accused most American critics of being equally detrimental to the full development of a distinctive American literature:

> There is an American conspiracy in effect to keep hidden the disturbing idea that literature has been, is being and will be produced in this country. Among the "established" critics of the various literary journals there is a tacit agreement to up and clout every American who shows signs of producing anything approaching literary excellence. If he is bad enough to insure his

dropping out of sight within a month or so, they pass him a generous meed of praise, conscious that he will not, in the future, arise and trouble them.

It may be the enchantment of distance; it may be the almost universal habit of acquiring matters of intellect and taste at second hand. Certain it is that an inferior Russian, French or English writer can be assured deference from our native critics, while a worthy American can expect only a snub. According to their narrow lights of esthetic judgment, our native critics (excepting, here, such men as James Huneker, H. L. Mencken, John Macy and a few others) will rule an American writer out as immoral and incompetent and let in a foreign writer whose subject matter, technique and point of view are hardly to be differentiated from that of the outlawed American.[5]

Therefore, Rascoe urged more consideration for American writers, pointing out, as an example, that "H. L. Mencken, whose *A Book of Burlesques* strikes with fine precision many notes as fundamental as themes from Swift, Molière and Aristophanes, is unread save by a few and is avoided mention by those who write of books. But Stephen Leacock, a Canadian clown, whose burlesques are no more rereadable than the jokes of vaudeville, is invited to give lectures at American universities."[6]

Another way in which Rascoe tried to achieve his goal of winning recognition for American literature was to publicize what he considered to be good, genuinely American writing. Accordingly, after he had seen a production of Elmer Rice's *The Adding Machine* in 1923, he wrote that he "came away vastly impressed and enthusiastic.... It seems to me to be a genuine contribution to American drama, miles ahead of most foreign imitations which have been generously acclaimed." Rascoe commended Rice for his use of the American language and for his employement of "the American idiom with veracious and splendid effect...."[7] As another example, in 1925 he wrote a defense of American lyric poets, becoming lyrical over E. E. Cummings:

If there is a finer lyricist since Keats and Swinburne (I include them both), forgetting Yeats, in the English language I wish you would introduce me to him. Uneven? Yes, I grant you! So was God—look at Ben Turpin and the Siamese Twins! Even He is always experimenting and sometimes turning out things more fascinating than tasteful. Even He is more radical and revolutionary and whimsical than that of printing the first person singular

with a lower case "i"—look at His turning out a man like Volstead.
Take it all in all, or all in little, Cumming's poetry, the best of it,
is beauty like a lark's song or the Ode on a Grecian Urn or any
other danged thing you please. I won't argue the case any more.
When our myopic literary birchmen finally gutter out in the
grease of their own stupidities, when the geoffreys have left their
parsonage and all the reeds are broken and the putnams have
ceased to put—then milady, my dear lady, America will have discovered that it has some poets and Cummings will be highty-
tighty among the lot.[8]

Years later, as an editorial adviser for Doubleday, Doran,
Rascoe explained his aim to Louis Paul; he said that "... I
wouldn't be in this business five minutes if I did not believe that
I was fostering the cause of good literature and acting as a sort
of midwife to find work that is yet to come into being."[9] And he
explained elsewhere that he first attacked Ezra Pound—in 1917—
because Pound was undermining what he was trying to do: "My
first thrust at Pound in the Chicago Tribune was not a literary
criticism but a literary editorial, provoked by Pound's writings in
and letters to English reviews, writings which were not literary
criticism and not directed at me but scurrilous, epithetical attacks
against American writers, American reviews, America as a race
of barbarians. ... I believe Pound knew perfectly well that my
pride has been that I have been in the van in proclaiming meritorious work, fighting for the recognition of poets like Eliot, and
prose writers like Cabell and Dreiser when they were being
attacked or neglected."[10]

II *Combats Censorship*

Another of Rascoe's major contributions not mentioned by
Soskin was his vigorous, courageous fight against censorship,
which he considered to be specially pernicious to the cause of
good literature. Rascoe wrote many articles denouncing all forms
of censorship; as an example, in the late teens he wrote a strong
editorial entitled "Our Vicious Zeal" when the Society for the
Suppression of Vice, "our peculiarly American form of the In-
quisition," as Rascoe called the Society, seized Freud's mono-
graph on Leonardo da Vinci and brought its publishers into
court on the charge of "publishing and disseminating an immoral
book." Calling this "one more grotesque act of highhanded tyr-

anny," Rascoe pointed out that no doubt costly litigation would ensue, frightening publishers into refusing to publish "translated works of high scientific and literary value" or into the "bowdlerizing of others until they are scarcely more than scenarios of the original."[11]

And this censorship, Rascoe felt, would keep American literature "at the skimmed-milk consistency which makes us the laughing stock of civilized Europeans and the object of sneers even from the English, whose censorship is only a trifle less barbarous." He then pointed out how stupidly the Vice Society had behaved in suppressing Freud's work: "The Freud treatise, couched in a terminology intelligible only to educated adults, is seized by them two years after publication on the same grounds upon which they seized the world-renowned classics of Rabelais, Boccaccio, Balzac, Daudet, Thomas Hardy and Gautier . . . because it might 'excite impure thoughts in the minds of persons that are susceptible to impure thoughts' or 'tend to deprave the minds of the young and inexperienced,' or 'arouse a libidinous passion . . . in the mind of a modest woman.'" Rascoe then warned of the harmful effects of this kind of behavior on American literature:

> To all this pious naïveté, this confession of infantile mentality, this avowal of prepossession for smut and an interest in books solely dependent upon the erotic excitation to be got out of it, the artist, the critic, the scientist and the intelligent reader can only shrug in despair and wonder how much further the will of the illiterate, the obsessed-by-vice, the self-elected guardians of the welfare of others will be worked to reduce our literature to that which may be read in young ladies' seminaries without provoking giggles.
>
> The actual effect of all this pernicious activity has been, of course, to make the current reading matter and amusement in America unexampled in its nastiness as well as unique in its utter vacuity. Instead of the healthy obscenity of Rabelais and the frankly critical works of the French literary psychologists and the exquisite prose and poetic compositions of other countries, we have the discretely and hence emphatically pornographic—nudity clothed in a chemise and black silk stockings, bedroom farces, the Victory Loan poster of H. C. Christy, the Junior Leg Show, and the Follies, "a national institution." In this no other country is our equal. Our literature is for "the young and inexperienced" and for "modest women" to read—in secret.[12]

Rascoe then went on in this editorial to show also that censorship causes artists of other nations to "conform to our unhealthy inversion"; that many of the "unsurpassed novels of Anatole France, the works of French, Flemish, Dutch, Italian, Russian, Spanish and Scandinavian masters come to us expurgated, toned down, innocuous, ready for the nursery"; and that, even worse, "the work of unquestioned genius in other countries . . . remains untranslated (or unavailable to the public) for the very reason that such an enterprise is too dangerous to the publishers." He then concluded with a summary of the "net result of the activities" of the Vice Society: "it has forced literary masterpieces into a classification with the bawdy and obscene; it has turned many of our writers toward an unhealthy eroticism; and it has kept this nation the most ignorant of all civilized nations with the work of the genius of other countries."[13]

This attack against censorship, one of many, was extremely forceful, and no doubt effective. In writing these attacks, Rascoe frequently exposed himself to dangers from his readers, from his employers, and from his enemies. Though of course Rascoe's contribution to this struggle cannot be measured exactly, there is no doubt that he, along with Mencken and others of the literary radicals, contributed importantly to its favorable outcome.

III *Helps Other Writers*

A third contribution of Rascoe's in this "scrap he's fighting for letters,"[14] as Galantière put it, was to give special help to many writers. Galantière, for one, in pointing out his own indebtedness to Rascoe, told Rascoe that "Except for that job [writing a Paris literary letter for the *New York Tribune*] for which no one else would conceivably have engaged me—I should be utterly unkown in New York today. It brought me kudos and friends and a few other jobs, and I don't need to tell you how much indebted to you I feel." Galantière also told Rascoe that ". . . except for you I should be a nonentity in literary journalism instead of the possessor of a slight reputation."[15]

As editor of various publications Rascoe provided a forum (and pay) for many writers. Dreiser, to cite an unusual example, was asked by the editor of the *New York World* to write an article on the subject of divorce and to "make some comment on

the New York State law which allows divorce on only one ground
—adultery." The pay would be two hundred dollars. Dreiser
wrote the article and submitted it to Paul Palmer, the *World's*
Sunday Editor, "who read it and expressed himself as highly
pleased with it and in sympathy with the opinions expounded,
but interposed an objection to a paragraph containing the sentence: 'Not only that, but that world's largest real estate organization, the Catholic Church condemns them to hell besides. As
though one hell weren't enough.' From this he wished to delete
the phrase '*that world's largest real estate organization*' saying it
would be offensive to Catholic readers."[16]

Dreiser in a letter explaining this situation to Rascoe said: "I
replied that I objected to the removal of that particular phrase,
since I was writing a frank statement of my beliefs for all the
people and not writing with a view to catering to or placating
the Catholic Church." He said that he told Palmer either to take
the article with the phrase for two hundred dollars or without
the phrase for five hundred dollars, that the "total contribution of
The World to the welfare of the Catholic Church" would be three
hundred dollars.[17] Palmer, in refusing Dreiser's offer, wrote that
"I will be unable to print your divorce article with the phrase
'that world's largest real estate organization' included."[18] Dreiser's
answer to Palmer was that he hoped that the *World* would be as
careful of the feelings of all other organizations and individuals
—large and small—or "as tender" as Palmer was being to the
Catholic Church; and he told Palmer, "I am returning the check.
Please return the article."[19] At that time Rascoe was associate
editor of *Plain Talk,* and he took Dreiser's article and printed it
in that publication under the title, "Whom God Hath Joined
Together. . . ." And Rascoe used the article exactly as Dreiser had
written it, including the "offensive phrase."[20]

In recognition of Rascoe's help to him, Dreiser presented
Rascoe with copy number five of the first edition (limited to 795
copies) of *An American Tragedy.* In this presentation copy
Dreiser wrote: "Dear Rascoe: I want you to have this. Will you
accept it with my earnest thanks for your various services in my
behalf[?] Theodore Dreiser[.]"[21] Cabell also wrote to thank
Rascoe for his efforts in behalf of Cabell's work; Cabell wrote
that "My debt to you is vast. I shall never forget that fact: . . ."[22]
And Cabell dedicated *Jurgen* to Rascoe in 1919.

Rascoe's help to writers was both frequent and diverse. Dreiser, again, for example, he helped in many ways: in 1921 he helped Dreiser edit *Newspaper Days*, he advised Dreiser on certain books to read, and he constantly supported Dreiser in his battle against Philistinism. After a movie based on *An American Tragedy* had been made—which Dreiser thought was so false to his book that he wanted to prevent its being released—Dreiser invited Rascoe (among other critics) to a private viewing of the movie to get his opinion about it. The very next day Rascoe advised Dreiser on the movie: "My opinion of 'An American Tragedy' in the motion picture version shown to us yesterday is that it is just another motion picture and not even an approach to a translation of the novel in terms of the motion pictures. Even as an ordinary movie it is doomed to be a terrific box-office failure as it now stands. For a popular audience it is deficient in precisely that emotional content which made the novel so great a success. Few people would have read 'An American Tragedy' if the hero had been presented in as unsympathetic a light as he is presented in the motion picture version." Rascoe then commended Dreiser for his stand: "You are making history—as you have done before—in art and literature by your conscientious stand in this matter. It may mean the artistic (and financial) redemption of the motion picture business. And it certainly means re-defining the relationship between the author of a novel and the motion picture firm which exploits the success of that novel, as a novel, by adapting it for the screen."[23]

Alfred Kreymborg, whose work Rascoe had first praised in 1919 in Chicago, also expressed his indebtedness to Rascoe. While literary critic for *Esquire*, Rascoe attended a Ziegfeld show in which he heard Jimmy Durante recite Kreymborg's "One-Room-Two-Room" poem. Later Rascoe saw Kreymborg on the street and congratulated him on selling the poem to Durante. Kreymborg told Rascoe that he did not know anything about it; that he did not have enough money to buy a ticket to the show. In an article in *Esquire* Rascoe "roasted hell" out of Durante for stealing the poem, and Kreymborg sued Durante. Robert Benchley objected, saying that an "obscure Village poet should be proud to have his stuff exploited by the great artist Durante."[24] Rascoe then wrote an article in *Esquire* attacking Benchley's article. Kreymborg wrote to Rascoe about this article: "What a gorgeous article! What a slaughter of boobies! What a defense of friends and artists! What a boy, what a guy, what a man! And what a judge by Jesus! Has the bench replied, and the Benchley?"[25] Later Kreymborg wrote Rascoe again, saying that ". . . I've a notion I owe my debut in Esquire to your article on the Schnozzle."[26]

But Rascoe's greatest help to individual writers was of a different kind. Galantière recognized this help when he said to Rascoe that ". . . I remember very well thinking from Paris, as I read the *Daybook* in those years, that you were bringing [Edmund Wilson] wonderfully to the attention of a public that would never know about him except through you. . . ."[27] In other words, Rascoe used his position as editor, critic, and columnist to publicize worthy but little recognized writers. That, he said in 1920, was precisely the reason that in 1917 he had written "Fanfare"— to bring "Mencken to the attention of the public": ["Fanfare"] "was hortatory rather than expository and its aim was to increase, so far as possible, Mr. Mencken's audience. He had not at that time the following he now enjoys; and his importance as a literary figure, while just as real, was not then so apparent as it is now."[28]

IV   *Recognizes Unknown Writers*

Furthermore, Rascoe often used his columns to call attention to the work of unknown writers. For example, he wrote in 1929 in his column in *Plain Talk* about Graham Greene's first novel that "Without any hesitancy whatever I would recommend to your attention *The Man Within* (Doubleday, Doran) by Graham Greene. The author is a newcomer. This is his first novel. He is a young English man. . . . When he wishes to create a mood he knows how to handle the rhythm of his sentences in the proper way—a trick he may have learned from Stevenson. His style, however, is his own, and it is a style of power and distinction." Rascoe predicted greatness for Greene: "Graham Greene has something of Dostoievsky's ability to explore the secret recesses of the soul. His first novel is a mature and beautiful piece of work. He will, I predict, become a conspicuous figure in the field of English fiction."[29]

In another of his "Daybook" columns in 1931 he wrote about Kay Boyle's first novel, *Plagued by the Nightingale*, that "It is a novel to be purchased, read and kept against the time when it will command a premium on the first edition; for Miss Boyle is almost certain to distinguish herself brilliantly. For several years Miss Boyle's apprentice pieces in prose have been appearing in the Tendenz magazines like 'transition,' and her work has also appeared in The American Caravan, a miscellany of prose and poetry from the newer writers whose work is avocados to the general. There is a hardness of mind behind the feline grace of her style and a piquant novelty in her descriptive method."[30]

It would be impossible to mention all of the unrecognized writers that Rascoe wrote about, but this was a large part of his accomplishment. Of course, he was wrong in his judgment about many of these writers (he was also right about many of them); but for a recognized critic just to take notice of their work surely provided inspiration for many of these writers. One of the writers to whom Rascoe's early encouragement had meant much was Louis Paul, who wrote to Rascoe that

> When I first visited you, you were genuinely interested in me and not in creating in me a phony picture of yourself as the condescending litterateur. I get a different picture of the litterateur, Burton. Your instinct is to detect those first faint and to the rest of us quite imperceptible flowerings which indicate the future writer of talent. I think to bring a lad along a few steps on this tough literary road gives you an intense pleasure entirely divorced from either what you may achieve in prestige as a discoverer of talent, or financial reward . . . ; yet you go right on pulling 'em up from the minors, so to speak, and enjoying it. No, I've a different picture of the writer. No writer (and this definitely includes myself) has value to me until he has demonstrated over a period of years his ability to present a full canvas painted with his own peculiar temperatment. . . . Sure, this is playing it pretty safe. . . . This is why I was so thoroughly amazed when, merely from 'Jedwick,' you predicted I was a writer. How in hell could you know.[31]

Esquire had published "Jedwick," one of Paul's first stories, and Rascoe had praised it in his column.

Rascoe was probably the first critic in America to mention Hemingway's work in print. He noted in his "Day Book" column in the *New York Tribune* on October 14, 1923, that Edmund Wilson had "called my attention to some amusing stuff by Ernest Hemingway in the new issue of 'The Little Review.' Galantière sent me a copy of Hemingway's 'Three Stories and Ten Poems,' which was published in Paris, and said that I would find it interesting, but I have not yet got around to reading it." He also wrote in his "Day Book" on June 15, 1924, the first appreciation of Hemingway's work in America. He wrote that "Wilson came back to the house with us and we sat up until after midnight talking. One of the writers we discussed was Ernest Hemingway, a young American resident of Paris, who has published two books, one of thumbnail short stories called 'In Our Time' and the other entitled, 'Three Stories and Ten Poems.' They are prose experiments showing the influence of both Ring Lardner and Sherwood Anderson, with here and there a sentence or a paragraph of genuine power. The pieces in 'In Our Time' are concisely dramatic and carry implications which start the reader's imagination. Here is a sample: ..."[32]

Hemingway first wrote Wilson on November 11, 1923, and began his letter with, "In Burton Rascoe's Social and Literary Notes I saw you had drawn his attention to some writing of mine ... ," referring to Rascoe's first mentioning Hemingway's work.[33] Wilson reviewed *In Our Time* and *Three Stories and Ten Poems* in *The Dial* of October, 1924; and Hemingway wrote to Wilson on October 18, 1924, to thank him for the review. In this letter, Hemingway made the statement that "Some bright boy said *In Our Time* was a series of thumbnail sketches showing a great deal of talent but obviously under the influence of Ring Lardner. Yeah!"[34] Hemingway's comment probably referred to Rascoe's appreciation in which he described *In Our Time* as "thumbnail short stories" and correctly pointed out the influences of Anderson and Lardner on Hemingway (though Hemingway denied the Lardner influence to Wilson). Rascoe later wrote a longer article on Hemingway which appeared in the November, 1925, issue of *Arts and Decoration,* and which was listed incorrectly by Louis Henry Cohn in his *Bibliography of Hemingway* as being the first extensive critical article ever to appear on Hemingway. It was the second; Wilson's review was the first.

V *Records His Times*

For his generous recognition of the worth of unknown writers alone, Rascoe deserves a place in the literary history of America—by 1935 eleven writers had dedicated books to him—but his writ-

ing is also an important and useful source for studying the social,
political, and literary history of the period that began for him
about 1916. As a literary critic and editor, and as an editorial
adviser to a large publisher, he was involved in and wrote about
many of the literary and cultural activities of the period. The
Boswellizations alone in the "Day Book" make it an excellent
source book on the 1920's. Malcolm Cowley has written in *Exile's
Return* of Rascoe's "Day Book" that ". . . his weekly book page in
the *New York Herald Tribune* . . . gave a better picture of that
frenzied age [the pre-depression 1920's] than any historian could
hope to equal. He was distinguished among literary journalists
by really loving his profession, by speaking with hasty candor and
being absolutely unself-protective in his hates and enthusiasms.
He attacked the men of swollen reputation, in spite of the pain
to them and the danger to himself (and eventually at the cost of
his job). He tried to discover and glorify the work of artists and
writers then unknown to the public—the good, bad, and indifferent ones. . . ."[35] Cowley also noted in *After the Genteel Tradition* in his "A Literary Calendar: 1911–1930" that in 1924 Rascoe
paid a penalty for his early work: "Burton Rascoe, friend of the
anti-genteel writers, loses his job as editor of the *Herald-Tribune
Books* and is replaced by Stuart Pratt Sherman, the academic
Humanist."[36] Losing his job was a repetition of what had happened earlier in Chicago, and it would happen again.

Rascoe's highly readable "Day Book" was extremely popular,
and as such it no doubt succeeded in enlarging the audiences of
Yeats, France, Dreiser, Stevens, Bodenheim, Aiken, Anderson,
and a whole host of neglected writers or of writers under attack.
Perhaps more significantly, however, Rascoe has here recorded
and preserved for posterity much interesting and valuable information. In his reports of conversations he had with many artists
and writers in the 1920's, he—owing largely to his photographic
memory—has saved material that otherwise would be lost forever.

One of hundreds of conversations he similarly recorded was
one in which Sherwood Anderson discussed how he had become
interested in Gertrude Stein, and how he believed that she was
behind the movement toward a new method of expression. He
then "quoted" Anderson's description of his reaction on first hear-
ing his brother, Karl Anderson the painter, reading aloud from
Stein's *Tender Buttons*:

... I got up dazed and left the room. I felt as if a door to a new world had opened for me. I walked about alone for half the night turning this new experience over in my mind. She seemed to me like a woman who played with words in the same way another person might toy with precious stones, admiring and being thrilled by them and letting them fall through her fingers to catch their changing color and radiance. I don't think she will ever be anything to readers but I think that she is a big event in literature, that she is of the utmost importance to writers. She gives them a new sense of word values. Expression had been formulated and without life and Gertrude Stein comes along and jumbles words all up and gives combinations of them new emotional values and meanings.

Rascoe reported Anderson's saying that he had later visited Stein in Paris and had found her

a big husky, sensible and amiable woman who might have been the wife of an Iowa horse doctor. She is so used to being made fun of and kidded about her work that she laughs about it and makes a joke of it herself; but just the same she takes herself seriously and she believes in her soul that her work is important. I learned this, when after I told her how seriously impressed and moved I had been by her work, she was immensely pleased. She showed me her unpublished work. There are piles of it, ... She has resigned herself apparently to being made the butt of a joke but all the time she is doing work which will, some day, be shown to have a tremendous influence upon literary expression. A thousand years from now writing will be vastly different from what it is now, and I believe that it will be seen that these experiments by Gertrude Stein will have been back of it all, just as the experiments Cézanne made and threw or gave away are back of the whole modern movement in painting.[37]

This "Day Book" column was attacked in a literary editorial in The Literary Review of the *New York Evening Post*; both Rascoe and Anderson were criticized for lacking critical standards. In a subsequent "Day Book" column Rascoe defended both Anderson and Stein: "It may appear to the 'Literary Review' commentator that Miss Stein is a buffoon, but to me (after Mr. Anderson's report) and to Mr. Anderson she is not.... Knowledge has come to her that her experiments are of use rather to writers than to the general public, that in dissociating words and making new patterns of verbal suggestion and imagery she cannot hope to

evoke more than ridicule from the public and from the critics
who are hostile to new forms." Rascoe then admitted that he had
had little success in experiencing Stein's "word patterns," but
that to Anderson "they have been a revelation and an inspiration;
therein is their justification."[38]

An immense quantity of similar material appeared in Rascoe's
various newspaper and magazine columns, most of which has
never been reprinted in book form. His work before and during
the 1920's is especially rich in information about writers and writing. This vivid, short portrait of Dreiser at a dinner party given
by T. R. Smith in March of 1924 was never reprinted; it is typical
of much of the valuable material preserved in the Rascoe archives:

> Dreiser was very quiet, as usual, saying little throughout a long
> evening. He is a diffident man, only slowly to be drawn into a
> conversation, and even then he speaks hesitantly as if to depre-
> cate in advance what he has to say. He never seems bored; he
> follows mere badinage with an eagerness, even; but he seems
> incapable, when his audience is more than one, of freeing his
> opinions or releasing his isolated self. It is for that reason that he
> pours so much of himself into his books. He sits, neat, in loose
> gray tweeds, his grey eyes in a fixed expression of humility, tend-
> erness and compassion, and his curious thick-lipped mouth drawn
> up on one side to a sort of snarling smile that is something be-
> tween anguish and sardonic amusement. He looks a plodder
> and he is, of course; but with what singleness of purpose, with
> what magnificent, determination, with what a Golem-like stride![39]

VI *Criticizes the Critics*

Another important aspect of Rascoe's work was his insistence
on exposing error and on attacking books of criticism and literary
history which he thought were inimical to the cause of good
American literature and culture; he felt that "A critic's remarks
are not addressed to the author but to the public or to that portion of it which may or may not read the book under review. It is
too late to reason with an author after his book is published. The
damage is done. Unless the book is withdrawn to be rewritten or
revised, which is never done except under threat of prosecution,
it is out to make its way in the open market, however erroneous
its facts may be or however pernicious its effects may appear
to the reviewer."[40]

Thus when Grant C. Knight's *American Literature and Culture* was published, Rascoe said that he considered "it my function to warn readers against it." He began his attack by quoting these lines from Knight's book: "The first critic to break sharply with the American manner was James G. Hunecker [*sic*], a bohemian gentleman who not only liked to drink beer but also was not backward about admitting his tastes in his books. Hunecker came back to America from abroad to publicize certain foreigners now well known but then almost strangers to his countrymen: Shaw, Ibsen, Nietzsche, Strindberg, Stirner. At bottom a dilettante, Hunecker wrote enthusiastically about all the arts, the European arts, that is, for in common with most of his disciples he railed against American culture."

After chiding Knight for misspelling Huneker's name three times, and for giving Huneker a middle initial that he never used, Rascoe then accused Knight of being both wrong and ridiculous in his statements about Huneker: "I don't know whether it is considered reprehensible by a person like Mr. Knight for an author to admit he likes beer; but it does seem beyond belief to me that anybody should find anything peculiar about a critic's admitting his tastes in books." Rascoe then pointed out that Huneker had written twenty books, and a great amount of criticism of music and drama, including the editing of musical texts of Brahms, Strauss, Tchaikovsky, and Chopin; and he said that "In this entire amount of writing, if you find more than part of one short essay devoted to beer, and enough mentions of the beverage elsewhere to make up two printed pages I will eat Mr. Knight's book."

Rascoe then corrected the other statements of Knight's; and with running irony he accused Knight of bigotry:

Huneker did not come back to America "to publicize certain foreigners." Huneker went abroad to study music and, having completed his education, returned to America as a pianist, a teacher of music and a writer on musical subjects. He taught music for six years after returning to America before he became established as a music critic. His first book, "Mezzotints in Modern Music," was published fifteen years after his return from abroad and his next three books, "Chopin" (1900), "Melomaniacs" (1902) and "Overtones" (1904), were not devoted to publicizing the "certain foreigners" Mr. Knight mentions but to musical subjects and personalities.

It was not until the publication of "Iconoclasts" (1905) that Huneker began to write about those "certain foreigners now well known but then almost strangers to his countrymen," and that book helped to introduce to this country the work of Henrik Ibsen, Gerhart Hauptmann and Bernard Shaw. In introducing the work of these "certain foreigners," Huneker, even if he did nothing else, is entitled to the respect of any one with enough sense to pour water out of a boot.

If I were an English teacher I would flunk any pupil of mine who wrote a sentence like Mr. Knight's third one. It is not only sloppy; it is untrue. Huneker never "railed against American culture." That is the curious thing about Huneker. The occasion certainly presented itself for him to do so, but he never did. He chose another and more gracious method: he wrote about Tolstoi, Turgenev, Stendhal, Anatole France, Baudelaire, de Gourmont, Conrad, Huysmans, Schnitzler, d'Annunzio, Cézanne, Matisse, Vermeer, Ibsen, Shaw, Hauptmann, Strindberg, Nietzsche and the great masters of modern music in an infectiously enthusiastic manner, instead of wasting his time deriding the provincial taste then prevailing in America for Elbert Hubbard, the Rubaiyat, Howard Chandler Christy, Henry van Dyke and the Indian Love Lyrics.[41]

Finally, Rascoe noted that Knight had dismissed Huneker in thirteen silly lines but had given "fourteen lines of fulsome praise" to V. F. Calverton, "one of the most brilliant men to enter the field of criticism." Rascoe said that he respected Calverton's work, but that he felt certain that Calverton himself would be embarrassed by this account of American literary history.

Likewise, when a book was published that Rascoe thought was good for the cause of American literature, he introduced it to his readers; and so, for example, when Ludwig Lewisohn's *Expression in America* was published in 1932 he enthusiastically reviewed it. He began by saying that Lewisohn's book was "of almost sensational consequence," because Lewisohn

is a critic who has more nearly emancipated himself from the genteel tradition in discussing the classics of the language than any one I can recall. By this I mean that he has said what he thinks and knows and feels rather than said what it is the convention to say. This is very rare. Not even the most iconoclastic or irreverent critic like H. L. Mencken or the most nihilistic critic like Joseph Wood Krutch, for instance, has escaped the dead hand of what-is-the-right-thing-to-say, and it is the thing that gives a clammy quality to work of men like Paul Elmer More.

Lewisohn's achievement, Rascoe pointed out, was that he had
dramatically and movingly related "the long process of our eman-
cipation from the false critical values which dissociated art and
life and made of the bulk of our literature for a long period a
hollow performance, varied only by the occasional appearance of
an authentic artist." And, furthermore, Lewisohn's contentions
were precisely those of Rascoe's—that America had just entered
its "great period," and that within the last twenty years "we have
grown out of our infantile stage in ideas and expression." Rascoe
did find one "conspicuous lack" in Lewisohn, however:

> . . . he hasn't a good appreciation of either wit or humor. He is
> almost totally lacking in a sense of humor himself, which is not a
> handicap, except in so far as it limits his capacity to enjoy a very
> important department of literary expression. It leads him astray in
> his discussion of Mark Twain and Cabell; and it causes him to
> say, that H. L. Mencken's "best satiric pieces are among the best
> in the world. They rank him with Juvenal and Dryden." The first
> sentence is correct, but Mencken's humor, as revealed in his bur-
> lesques, is miles above the bilious, slimy, envious trash of Juvenal
> and much better stuff than Dryden's satire, athough he is com-
> parable to Dryden as a stylist. This is one of the few occasions
> where Mr. Lewisohn drops into the old academic trick of trying
> to heighten the luster of a living writer by comparing him favor-
> ably with, say, a writer like Juvenal who, rather unaccountably,
> has survived as a figure in Latin literature.[42]

Yet Lewisohn's book, Rascoe emphasized in concluding, was an
"event"; and he also suggested that "it comes at the right time,
too, because the free play of the creative spirit is in danger of
being caught between the dogmas of Fascism and Communism."
    Predictably, then, when Bernard De Voto's *Mark Twain's
America* was published that same year Rascoe praised it as being
"a rich and enjoyable book" which "should do much toward
emancipating American writers from the blighting hand of the
genteel tradition." He then discussed De Voto's book, noting that
"In writing this book Mr. De Voto has the audacity to use (most
of the time) good vigorous American prose, a prose which I
might say is quite distinct from that of the editorials of the London Spectator. There are signs all around nowadays that London
Spectator prose, while quite all right for the purposes of the edi-

tors of that weekly, is not the prose that is natural or native to Americans. Mr. De Voto is not only doing a great service to American letters. He is also, I believe, doing a service to the American people."[43] In writing this way about De Voto, Lewisohn, and many others, Rascoe felt—his work shows—that he was also in the service of American letters. He was.

VII *A Judicious Evaluator*

Later critics have tended to dismiss Rascoe as a literary critic chiefly because of his championship of Cabell. They reason from the false premise that, since he unreservedly championed Cabell, Rascoe was not a good critic. But, in so writing, they forget one thing—that one of Rascoe's chief aims as a critic was to win recognition for worthy but unknown American writers. And, more than anyone else, he did this for Cabell. Cabell had already published several novels, by 1917 when Rascoe first read *The Cream of the Jest* and excitedly reviwed it; yet Cabell was still almost completely unkown. This was the beginning of Rascoe's championship of Cabell's work which ultimately, when *Jurgen* was suppressed, became a *cause célèbre*.

As literary editor of the *Chicago Tribune* Rascoe was able in many ways to help Cabell, but obviously his aims extended beyond that. In defending Cabel, he engineered battles in Chicago and participated very much in a larger critical war that soon spread throughout the country—a warfare that led to a valuable re-examination of the quality and standards of American literature. Furthermore, just as this critical war in Chicago spread to other parts of the country, so too did the battle over the merits of Cabell spread to the merits of other writers. Thus, in a real sense, Rascoe used Cabell to gain recognition for many other American writers. And this feat, his writing proves, was as much his intention, his announced plan, as was his intention to discover and defend Cabell. Rascoe's ultimate importance, then, should be judged in the light of this intention.

From this point of view Rascoe becomes an important figure— he successfully helped to promote a distinctive American literature before and during the 1920's, a literature which he felt to be superior to a great deal of the English literature being offered to the American public at that time. This second- or third-rate

English stuff, Rascoe believed, was not only immoral, it was depriving much better American writers of an audience, of recognition, and of support. And so Rascoe was determined to combat this situation. This explains why he was so vociferous and, at times, so uncritical in his battles, even at times downright unjust, and also why he was willing to put forth so much energy, effort, and words into defending Cabell and others whom he believed Americans should know and honor. Cabell was an American. He was a better writer than many of the recognized "successful" English writers who were enjoying huge American receptions, such as Mrs. Humphry Ward, Marie Corelli, Hall Caine, and Robert Nichols; he was also a better writer than most of the popular American writers of the period—Harold Bell Wright, Eleanor H. Porter, Gene Stratton Porter, Winston Churchill, and Samuel Merwin. So, by using Cabell as a lever, Rascoe hoped to help lift American literature to a high enough standard so that cheap English (and American) literature would be de-emphasized, forgotten, or ignored.

In doing this, Rascoe certainly was noisy in his praise of many American writers. And if to us now he seemed to be uncritical, we must remember that it was partly his praise, or overpraise, or at least his early recognition of these American writers, that helped to bring our own literature to its now world-famous level. What really was needed then was, as John Chamberlain called it, an "eye-opener." Rascoe saw this. Critics like Stuart Pratt Sherman who attacked Dreiser and Mencken unmercifully (and just as uncritically) did not. For this work Rascoe rarely receives the credit he deserves because it—his greatest contribution to his age —was intangible and even now is nearly forgotten or has been obscured or distorted by others.

Furthermore, the record shows that Rascoe was aware of Cabell's deficiencies, and also of the deficiencies of the many other writers whom he championed. He wrote of these faults frequently. He wrote of the highly praised Joseph Hergesheimer's *The Party Dress*, for example, that Hergesheimer in certain passages in the book "has not felt the urge to improve upon the method and manner of the feminine masters of swooning fiction of the late 'eighties of American letters,'" and that "his appreciation of the subtleties of feminine charm when that charm is almost wholly artificial and characterless, and his ability as a moralist in defense of a decorum . . . is somewhat New Humanistic."[44] And in *We Were Interrupted* he explained that ". . . I was severe in my strictures on Dreiser's work when he turned away from fiction and imagined that he was a thinker, and . . . I was very severe with the young writers when their work fell off in quality. Of F. Scott Fitzgerald's second book I wrote, 'The trouble with *The Beautiful and Damned* . . . is that it is blubberingly sentimental.' " Rascoe said in this review that Fitzgerald has "not matured at all" but rather had collapsed "into the banal and commonplace."[45]

Finally, Rascoe was right about Cabell: Cabell *at that time* was one of the best *writers* in America. All of those writers who originally praised Cabell—Mencken, Sinclair Lewis, Fitzgerald, Hergesheimer, Glasgow, Dreiser, Cather, and many of the best critics of the time—thought so too. Though Rascoe was in large measure responsible for their praise of Cabell, they all thought of Cabell as a *writer*. Rascoe's first concern was esthetic; he praised Cabell most for his use of satire, irony, and wit—that is, for his style, not so much for the content of his works, about which Rascoe often expressed his disapproval. Only a few years ago Perry Miller praised even the content of *Jurgen*: "Those who remember the noise about the book, or those who merely make researches into that vanished era, can cherish the sense which Cabell diffused of wit, detachment, and of sophistication that America had long dreamed of but supposedly never yet attained. A younger reader, not cognizant of the provinciality of that sweet epoch, may find it difficult to imagine wherein 'Jurgen' gave offense. Such a one had better read the work attentively, for the fact remains that 'Jurgen,' despite its stylistic affections, is still scandalous and still delicious."[46] Thus, for the most part, Rascoe was a judicious critic of the American writers whom he championed.

Therefore, Rascoe's chief importance was to his own times, and perhaps, now, to an understanding of his times. His influence on his age was both pervasive and direct. As an editor and critic he played an important part in helping to make the young American literature grow up in the sparse cultural soil that was America in the second and third decades of this century. Also, much of his criticism was sound; and his style and ironic humor may even still be read for enjoyment.

VIII *Critical Limitations and Deficiencies*

There are some valid reasons, of course, for Rascoe's decline, and these reasons should also be mentioned in evaluating his contributions. Among these must be counted his limitations and deficiencies as a critic. First, he was divided in mind and role— he was a skeptic and an optimist, an idealist and a realist, a conservative and a liberal; he was an editor and an author, a journalist and a critic. He was vain and, especially in his latter years, extremely egotistical; yet he could be kind and humble. And temperamentally, at least, he was scholarly and conservative; but, in his aims, techniques, and methods, he belonged with the literary radicals. All of these contraries of character and personality took their toll on him as a disciplined writer and critic. He simply never integrated himself into one effective, positive force.

Second, the virtue of his being a good journalist and editor hurt him as a critic. His journalistic and editorial work took too much of his time and energy away from his work as a critic. And even the best journalists and editors are soon forgotten. He once told Cabell that "I hate to spread my energies so much. I wish I could give up editing altogether but my expenses are heavy and I see no other way out."[47] Thus much of Rascoe's work became mere journalism, and it deserves to be forgotten. He wrote too much— in his weekly or monthly columns year after year—and consequently sacrificed much to expediency; even in his best work his carelessness in the use of language and syntax (resulting from the careless newspaper habit of haste) and his journalistic style are evident. He had a keen awareness of what was (or could be made into) literary news; but the haste of writing for newspapers and the habits contracted while mass-producing criticism for a deadline left a permanent mark on his work. He had to pay this price for cheapening his art during the decisive years of his development.

A third reason for Rascoe's neglect today is that he did not grow or change much as a critic after the middle 1920's; and his belief in the validity of only subjective criticism weakened and limited the range and depth of his literary criticism. Although he was intellectual and even scholarly, criticism remained for him essentially the expression of his personality. The result of this trait was, of course, that he often came to use the same superficial material over and over again, and drearily to say the same thing again and again, and to contradict himself, or to change his mind numerous times. Nor did his critical methods change much. Consequently, his later work in his columns is almost unreadable now and militates against his earlier important work.

Finally, he spent too much of his time in one controversy after another: defending American literature and writers, attacking the "genteel" critics, academicism, censorship, New Humanism, and, beginning in the 1930's, attacking the radical political advocates. Though he was on the winning side in most of these important battles, when a battle is over hardly any one ever remembers even the combatants, no matter how hard the battles were or who won.

In *We Were Interrupted* Rascoe wrote correctly that "I suspect that few of the writers of the present generation, who enjoy a relative freedom of expression, realize how tough the battle was and how long prolonged, twenty-odd years ago, that enabled them to present their vision of life with honesty and without fear."[48] Also, many others fought alongside Rascoe in these battles and shared in the victories; and some, Rascoe felt, in an effort to enhance their own reputations, have failed to show gratitude in print for his efforts in their behalf, or have even distorted the historical record.[49]

Notes and References

Chapter One

1. *Before I Forget* (New York, 1937), pp. 16–56.
2. All notebooks, diaries, journals, correspondence, manuscripts, typescripts, newspaper clippings, and the manuscript of *Gustibus* are in the Burton Rascoe Collection in the Rare Book Collection of the Library of the University of Pennsylvania. Hereafter cited as BRC.
3. BRC.
4. *Before I Forget*, pp. 100–103, 139–41.
5. Diary, March 15, 1910.
6. Journal, June 1, 1910.
7. *Before I Forget*, pp. 149–52.
8. *Ibid.*, pp. 145–49. Selections from this early column are reprinted in *Before I Forget*, pp. 379–81.
9. *Ibid.*, p. 175.
10. *Ibid.*, p. 176.
11. *Ibid.*, p. 230.
12. Alfred Kazin, *On Native Grounds* (New York, 1942), pp. 175–76.
13. See letter from Elia W. Peattie to Rascoe, February 9, 1918; see also "Rascoe," in unpublished typescript, "Chicago's Golden Age in Life and Letters," 1956, p. 6 (both, BRC).
14. *Before I Forget*, p. 311.
15. Bernard Duffey, *The Chicago Renaissance in American Letters: A Critical History* (East Lansing, 1954), p. 257.
16. "Personal Ethics Without Sweetmeats," *Chicago Tribune,* books sec., p. 9.
17. Willard Huntington Wright, Letter, April 7, 1916.
18. Wright, Letter, April 30, 1920.
19. *We Were Interrupted* (New York, 1947), p. 33.
20. Rascoe told Harry Hansen in a letter on July 23, 1924, that for two years he read practically nothing else but the French moderns.
21. Letter to James Branch Cabell, October 20, 1919.
22. *Before I Forget*, pp. 370–72.
23. H. L. Mencken, Letter, May 6, 1920. W. A. Swanberg in his *Dreiser* (New York, 1965) makes several egregious errors when he says that Rascoe was with the *New York Tribune* in 1919 (pp. 235–36). Rascoe was with the *Chicago Tribune* until 1920. He went to the *New York Tribune* in 1922 and was succeeded in 1924 by Stuart P. Sherman, not in 1919 by Burton Kline, as Mr. Swanberg says.
24. George Jean Nathan, Letter, May 7, 1920.

25. Income Tax Returns, BRC.

26. Letter to Percy Hammond, May 6, 1926.

27. Letter to Rascoe's mother, June 10, 1932.

28. *We Were Interrupted*, pp. 79–80.

29. *Ibid.*, p. 104.

30. *Ibid.*, p. 120.

31. *Ibid.*

32. *Ibid.*

33. *Ibid.*, pp. 122–23.

34. *Ibid.*, p. 125.

35. Letter to Cabell, May 18, 1922.

36. *We Were Interrupted*, p. 130.

37. Ernest Hemingway, Letter to Edmund Wilson, November 25, 1923—quoted by Wilson in *A Literary Chronicle: 1920–1950* (Garden City, New York, 1956), p. 43.

38. Harry Hansen, Letter, September 29, 1947.

39. Edmund Wilson, *A Literary Chronicle: 1920–1950* (Garden City, 1956), pp. 83–84.

40. Victor Llona, "La Littérature Française jugée par les grands écrivains étrangers Burton Rascoe," *Le Journal Littéraire,* January 31, 1925, p. 9. (My translation.)

41. Letter to Dreiser, June 1, 1926. Theodore Dreiser Collection, University of Pennsylvania Library.

42. Lewis Galantière, Letter, July 15, 1926.

43. "A Salute to Youth," *The Daily Maroon,* University of Chicago, Celebrities Number, 1927, p. 11.

44. Letter to Cabell, April 26, 1927.

45. Letter to Dreiser, September 8, 1927. Dreiser Collection.

46. Letter to David Smart, June 30, 1936; see also *We Were Interrupted,* p. 261.

47. Robert E. Spiller *et al., The Literary History of the United States* (New York, 1948; vol. 3, p. 62) incorrectly gives the dates of Rascoe's editorship of *The Bookman* as 1928–29.

48. "A Bookman's Day Book," *New York Sun,* April 9, 1932, p. 25.

49. Letter to Cabell, December 14, 1936.

50. Unsent application, BRC.

51. Rascoe wrote this in a marginal note on a clipping (BRC) of "The Libel Racket," by Ernest Sutherland Bates, which appeared in *The Modern Monthly,* December, 1937. He told Louis Paul in a letter January 25, 1938, that he felt that he was "conducting an important crusade for the little author without resources for freedom of speech and for the publisher as well." But later, after the suit had been settled, he saw that he had been quixotic—that neither the publishers nor authors cared about or even knew about what he was trying to do; he

explained in a letter to Louis Paul on January 23, 1940, the "shellacking" that he took because of the Annenberg suit and its consequence: "I am about as broke as I have ever been since I first took up the business of writing. . . ."

52. Letter to David Smart, September 7, 1937.
53. *Newsweek*, XI (April 25, 1938), 30.
54. " 'Scholars' Mugg the Camera," *Newsweek*, XI (April 25, 1938), 30.
55. Donald A. Roberts and Edith Hamilton, "This Will Never Do," letters to the editor column, *The Saturday Review of Literature*, IX (December 31, 1932), 357–58, 360. Miss Hamilton reprinted her letter in *The Ever-Present Past* (New York, 1964), pp. 120–26.
56. Typescript, BRC.
57. "Mencken, Nathan and Cabell," *The American Mercury*, XLIX (March, 1940), 368.
58. "Caldwell Lynches Two Negroes," *The American Mercury*, XLIX (April, 1940), 493–95. On May 8, 1940, Rascoe wrote to Louis Paul that "You wouldn't know it, of course, but TEMPORARILY, I am licked in New York by the Richard Wrights and Kip Fadimans. I've got enough sense to realize this and to gird up the old loins."
59. "Negro Novel and White Reviewers," *The American Mercury*, L (May, 1940), 115.
60. "Wolfe, Farrell and Hemingway," *The American Mercury*, LI (December, 1940), 493.
61. Letter to Van Wyck Brooks, September 9, 1940.
62. On June 30, 1940, Rascoe had written to Louis Paul that "Lyons and I are in utter disagreement (he being a rabid interventionist and wishing us to take up arms against Hitler at once and I being an equally rabid isolationist)–. . . ." And in another letter to Paul later (April 23, 1941) Rascoe explained why he had resigned from *The American Mercury* and what it had meant to him: "When Eugene Lyons refused to print a piece of mine (which later appeared in [']Common Sense' called 'Ladies Who Want Hell' and concerned with Dorothy Thompson, Claire Boothe and Edna Millay[)], I naturally told him I couldn't write for him any more. That cut $125 a month off my income, which used not to seem to amount to much but now does." He said that he was now unable to make a living selling articles to magazines because of his anti-British views.
63. This story had been shortened and reprinted in *Reader's Digest*, XXXVII (November, 1940), 89–90. This story earned Rascoe $400, he told Louis Paul in a letter on April 23, 1941, "which is just $100 less than Doubleday-Doran paid me outright for *Joys of Reading*, which has had a distribution of 125,000 copies."
64. Letter to Cabell, June 6, 1946.

65. Letter to Rascoe from Paul Dawson Eddy, President of Adelphi College, January 24, 1949; Rascoe was appointed Special Lecturer in the English Department.

Chapter Two

1. *We Were Interrupted*, pp. 152–53.
2. *Before I Forget*, p. xii. This preface was printed in *Wings* (June, 1937) as "Reflections on the Aim and Intention of *Before I Forget*."
3. Harry Hansen, Letter, May 9, [1924?].
4. Letter to Edward Bjorkman, September 20.
5. *Titans of Literature* (New York, 1932), p. 487.
6. "Some Impressions of Hergesheimer and of 'Java Head,'" *Chicago Tribune*, March 8, 1919, books sec., p. 9.
7. "Day Book," *New York Herald Tribune Books*, July 13, 1924, p. 26.
8. "History," typescript (BRC) of an article Rascoe was commissioned to write for *The English Journal*, but which was returned to Rascoe on September 14, 1933, by W. Wilbur Hatfield, editor of *The English Journal*, because it was too "philosophical." Hatfield asked Rascoe to write another article on "history which is literature." Rascoe later sent "History" to Stringfellow Barr, editor of *The Virginia Quarterly*, who wrote to Rascoe on October 28, 1933, that ". . . I like the article and want to publish it immediately." He requested that Rascoe first make certain revisions in the article, but Rascoe was never able to revise the article so that it was acceptable to Barr.
9. Letter to Cabell, December 20, 1933.
10. Letter to Dreiser, May 8, 1934. Dreiser Collection.
11. Letter to Milo Sutliff, December 13, 1947.
12. Letter to Victor Gollancz, May 21, 1935.
13. "Day Book," *New York Herald Tribune Books*, April 24, 1924. Reprinted as "Reminiscences of Georg Brandes" in *A Bookman's Daybook* (New York, 1929), pp. 227–28.
14. "Day Book," *New York Tribune Books*, May 13, 1923.
15. *Ibid.*, October 24, 1923.
16. *Ibid.*, May 27, 1923, p. 23.
17. Introduction to *The Ballad of Reading Gaol*, by Oscar Wilde (New York, The Limited Editions Club Edition, 1937. Reissued by The Heritage Press, New York, n.d.), pp. iv–vi.
18. Manuscript (BRC) of Rascoe's unpublished book, "Better English, How to Speak It—How to Write It," 1949, p. 26.
19. "Dreiser Shakes the Potter's Hand," *Chicago Tribune*, October 11, 1919, books sec., p. 13.

20. Clipping (BRC) of Rascoe's column, "Presuming You Are Interested in Such Items," *Chicago Tribune,* n.d., but the Folletts' book was published in 1918.

21. Clipping (BRC) of "Henry B. Fuller," *Chicago Tribune,* n.d., but Fuller's novel appeared in 1918.

22. Clipping (BRC) of newspaper article, n.p., n.d., but probably written in the early 1920's.

23. "Mr. Hecht's 'Gargoyles,'" *New York Tribune Books,* September 24, 1922, p. 7.

24. Typescript (BRC) of a review of Upton Sinclair's *Money Writes!* (1927).

25. "Literature Marches On!" (typescript, BRC), n.d., but internal evidence indicates that it was written in the early 1930's.

26. "Those Who Can, Criticize," *The Bookman,* LXVI (February, 1928), 671–72. A group review of books by Sir Edmund Gosse, J. B. Priestley, and H. L. Mencken.

27. "Day Book," *New York Tribune Books,* December 23, 1922. Reprinted in *A Bookman's Daybook* (New York, 1929) as "James Harvey Robinson," pp. 57–59.

28. "Day Book," *New York Tribune Books,* April 20, 1923.

29. In a letter to Rascoe on September 26, 1922, Buchanan had stated his reasons for disagreeing. Buchanan's letter also shows the reaction to subjective criticism that Rascoe felt was already beginning. Buchanan wrote that indulging in this "I like" business could only lead to stultification because the critic puts himself before what he is writing about. "You are exploiters of art. . . . For my part, I think it's darn fascinating. But it isn't criticism." He explained: "The present wave of subjective criticism can put up a rattling good argument for itself, but in the long run there's nothing to it; and our Menckens and Nathans and all the rest of them can argue themselves blue in the face without altering this fact one iota. The greatest mistake a critic can make is to confuse his reactions to the work with the work's intrinsic value. . . . The moment the critic capitulates to the easy lure of sheer likes and dislikes that moment is he headed for the cropper of inconsistency."

30. "Day Book," *New York Tribune Books,* November 12, 1922.

31. *Ibid.*

32. Typescript (BRC), n.d., but probably written in the early 1920's. Rascoe refers to Van Wyck Brooks's *Ordeal of Mark Twain* (1920) and other books of the early twenties, and the typescript was written on the back of *New York Herald Tribune* stationery.

33. "Day Book," *New York Tribune Books,* June 27, 1923, p. 22.

34. Clarence Day, Letter, February 12, 1925.

35. Lewis Galantière, Letter, March 20, [1925?]. Rascoe's portrait

of Cummings was published in his *Arts and Decoration* column after Rascoe's return from France where he had met Cummings. It was reprinted in *A Bookman's Daybook* (1929) as "Parisian Epilogue," pp. 297–305.

36. "Carl Sandburg," in *Before I Forget*, pp. 435–38. This article was first published in "The Literary Review" of the *New York Evening Post*, September 24, 1924, pp.1–2. Several of Rascoe's "Unconventional Portraits"—on Sherwood Anderson, Mencken, Joseph Hergesheimer, and Sandburg—were reprinted in Appendix IX of *Before I Forget*.

37. Lew Sarett, Letter, October 4, 1924.

38. Guy Holt, Letter, April 22.

39. "Prof. Sherman Gives Asylum To His Brood," *Chicago Tribune*, January 12, 1918. Reprinted in *Before I Forget*, Appendix VI, pp. 407–8. See Note 17 to Chapter III.

40. "Life of a Critic," *Plain Talk*, VI (January, 1930), 112.

41. *Ibid.*

42. The galley proofs and the originals of this correspondence are in the Rascoe Collection.

43. Letter to Cabell, April 9, 1937.

44. Letter to Cabell, May 24, 1937.

45. For a discussion of Sherman's method of argument, his racial views, attacks on him for these views by Ernest Boyd and J. E. Spingarn *et al.*, admissions by Zeitlin to Spingarn of Sherman's bias against critics of "alien origin," and of his personal attacks (namecalling), all after Rascoe's earlier attack on him for the same reasons, see the unpublished dissertation, "J. E. Spingarn and American Criticism," by L. Marshall Van Deusen, Jr., University of Pennsylvania, 1953, pp. 491–500.

46. Letter to Jacob Zeitlin, September 4, 1936.

47. There is a clipping of this *Chicago Daily News* attack in the Rascoe Collection.

48. "The Bible of the Nineties," *New York Tribune Books*, October 8, 1922, p. 7.

49. "Day Book," *New York Tribune Books*, August 22, 1922. Rascoe's use of the anagram Sarcoë Boturn (Burton Rascoe), whom he "quoted" in *Titans* (p. 163), indicates the personal nature of much of his criticism. In *Titans* (p. 278) he also stated that it was his métier "to put on record what he thinks, knows and feels."

50. *Titans*, p. 353.

51. *Titans*, pp. 384–85.

52. *Titans*, p. 389.

53. *Titans*, p. 485. Parody was a favorite method of Rascoe's; for example, in a review of Gertrude Stein's *Everybody's Autobiography*

he pretended to have a Japanese house boy review the book and thus was able to parody Stein's style: "Her avowal asserts that in the prolonging of thirty years incumbence in France she does not understand the French when they say it and that she does not peruse French books with aversion because there are no French books to read. She avows that everybody cultivates a facility in his natural language and that she has done this and no body else has and everybody else has." ("Self-Confidential," *The Saturday Review of Literature,* XVII [December 4, 1937], 11.)

54. Lewis Galantière, Letter, August 19, [1937]. Galantière was writing to Rascoe about *Before I Forget* which had just been published.

55. Galantière, Letter, June 10, [1937].

Chaper Three

1. "Here's a Chance to Own Another First Edition," *Chicago Tribune,* December 29, 1917, books sec., p. 9.

2. *Before I Forget,* p. 350.

3. "Here's a Chance to Own Another First Edition," p. 9.

4. Letter to Cabell, December 31, 1917.

5. Letter to Cabell, March 7, 1918.

6. Quoted by Rascoe in a letter to Cabell, April 23, 1918.

7. Several of these exchanges were reprinted in *Before I Forget,* pp. 386–95. For another discussion of the Cabell–Hughes fight see Padraic Colum and Margaret Freeman Cabell, eds., *Between Friends: Letters of James Branch Cabell and Others* (New York, 1962), pp. 45–50. Hughes attacked Cabell's romantic view that historical accuracy and realistic dialogue were not necessary in the novel.

8. Lewis Galantière, Letter, n.d., but sometime in April, 1918.

9. Letter to Galantière, April 18, 1918.

10. Letter to Cabell, January 5, 1920.

11. Conrad Aiken, Letters, February 17, February 18, and February 20, 1920.

12. Letter to Aiken, March 2, 1920.

13. Letter to H. L. Mencken, n.d.

14. "Fanfare," *Chicago Tribune,* November 11, 1917, books sec., p. 7. This article was later enlarged and revised by Mencken and Rascoe and issued in 1920 by Knopf as a publicity pamphlet: *Fanfare.* The pamphlet contained: Rascoe's "Fanfare," pp. 3–15; "The American Critic," by Vincent O'Sullivan, pp. 15–20; and a bibliography by F. C. Henderson, pp. 21–32. The article by O'Sullivan was from the London *New Witness,* November 28, 1919, pp. 30–32.

15. "Fanfare," p. 7.

16. In Edgar Kemler's *The Irreverent Mr. Mencken* (Boston,

1950), in a marginal note (BRC) at the beginning of Chapter 8, entitled "Bid for Immortality," Rascoe expressed himself on the Mencken trait of ingratitude which was discussed by Kemler in Chapter 8: "This whole chapter, I am constrained to feel, was the result of Mencken's reluctance to acknowledge any indebtedness to anyone as much as he was indebted to me for the campaign I waged in his behalf from 1917 through 1920 on the *Chicago Tribune,* when I was *the only* articulate and voluble champion and defender. This was an important factor in M's life, yet he ignored it." See also Note 49 to Chapter 5.

17. William Manchester, *Disturber of the Peace: The Life of H. L. Mencken* (New York, 1950), p. 102. In a marginal note (BRC) Rascoe commented on the "terrific" Sherman "blast": "Review entitled 'Prof. Sherman Gives Asylum to His Brood,' i.e., [his] collected *Nation* articles, *On Contemporary Literature.*"

18. Rascoe, Introduction, *The Smart Set Anthology,* edited by Rascoe and Groff Conklin (New York, 1934), pp. xxxiv–xxxv.

19. Marginal note by Rascoe on a clipping (BRC) of "Epitaph," probably written in 1949: "Whom he over-praised outrageously. G. was tenth-rate, but anti-Puritan, hence M's encomia."

20. Rascoe's note: "Now, in 1949, being said over and over again."

21. Rascoe's marginal note, probably written in 1949: "For the information of those who do not know what this means: René Ghil anticipated Rimbaud's Sonnet on the vowels—R. G. said vowels had identifying colors. And Mencken got the phrases quoted from Huneker's piece on Rimbaud, . . ."

22. "Notes for an Epitaph: H. L. Mencken," *New York Evening Post,* Literary Review, March 4, 1922, p. 461 (front page).

23. Vincent Starrett, "Burton Rascoe," typescript, n.d., BRC. Starrett's reference to Rascoe's "Epitaph" as being "recent" indicates that Starrett's article was written sometime early in 1922.

24. Joel E. Spingarn, Letter, March 5, 1922.

25. Alfred Kreymborg, Letter, March 30, 1922.

26. Mark Van Doren, Letter, October 22, 1924.

27. In 1955 Rascoe commented in a marginal note on a typescript of *Fanfare* (1920) about Alastair Cooke's Introduction to *The Vintage Mencken* (New York, 1955). He noted that Cooke "imagines he is the first to discover that Mencken was a humorist [and] not a thinker"; and then he argued with Cooke's statement, ". . . we can see that if he was overrated in his day as a thinker . . . , he was vastly underrated as a humorist." Rascoe wrote: "Cooke adduces no evidence, and I can think of none, that any critic, sympathetic or hostile, in the days of Mencken's emergence as a writer to be reckoned with or even at the height of the general acceptance of Mencken's importance in the American literature scheme, ever 'overrated' Mencken as a 'thinker'

although it is certainly true that Mencken's earliest antagonists—Sherman, Boynton, and other champions of the 'genteel' tradition—were insensible to Mencken's humor and so antagonistic to what they deemed vulgarity, coarseness, and lack of refinement that, far from 'under-rating' Mencken's humor and the merits of his style, they simply did not perceive that Mencken had either humor or style." Rascoe then pointed out how he had spoken specifically about Mencken's style and humor in "Fanfare," thirty-eight years before Cooke's discovery. He also pointed out how in 1922 in "Notes for an Epitaph: H. L. Mencken" he was the first to recognize and write about the decline in Mencken's influence, just when others were beginning to recognize and write about Mencken's influence.

28. Newton Arvin, "The Rôle of Mr. Mencken," *The Freeman*, VI (December 27, 1922), 381–82.

29. *Ibid.*, p. 382.

30. *We Were Interrupted*, pp. 148–49.

31. "A Residue of Reading," *New York Tribune Books*, September 3, 1922, p. 7; see also *We Were Interrupted*, pp. 148–50.

32. *We Were Interrupted*, pp. 149–50.

33. "In the Waste Land with Mr. Zane Grey," *New York Tribune Books*, January 21, 1923, p. 19.

34. "Day Book," *New York Tribune Books*, October 26, 1922.

35. "A Defense of T. S. Eliot," *A Bookman's Daybook*, edited by C. Hartley Grattan (New York, 1929), pp. 60–64.

36. *Ibid.*, p. 60.

37. "Day Book," *New York Tribune Books*, January 28, 1923, pp. 21, 26.

38. *Theodore Dreiser* (New York, 1925), Modern American Writers III.

39. G. D. Eaton, "A Lusty Howl from Tomb," *New York Morning Telegraph*, p. 7.

40. Letter to Seward Collins, November 16, 1929.

41. "*Humanism and America*," *Plain Talk*, VI (April, 1930), 497.

42. Edgar Lee Masters, Letter, March 11, 1930.

43. *We Were Interrupted*, p. 158.

44. "The New Humanists," *New York World*, April 20, p. 6.

45. "Pupils of Polonius," in *The Critique of Humanism*, edited by C. Hartley Grattan (New York, 1930), pp. 119, 126, 127.

46. O. W. Firkins, "Humanism at Bay," *The Saturday Review of Literature*, VII (June 14, 1930), 1124.

47. "A Bookman's Day Book," *New York Sun*, April 16, 1932, p. 18. Rascoe wrote, "I think 'Fifty Grand' is superb. Mr. Hemingway is a great artist. I thought I had been saying so ever since I first read his early experiments in short prose stories back in the old days of the Transatlantic Review."

48. Ezra Pound, "Pound to Rascoe," *New York Sun,* June 11, 1932, p. 36.

49. "Rascoe's Riposte," *New York Sun,* June 11, 1932, p. 36.

50. Maxwell Geismar, "Rascoe Returns to Memory Lane," *New York Times Book Review,* September 28, 1947, p. 3. Review of *We Were Interrupted.*

Chapter Four

1. Quoted by Rascoe in his unpublished typescript (BRC), "Chicago's Golden Age in Life and Letters," 1956. Rascoe also compiled the list of places where his work had been quoted.

2. Harry Hansen, "The First Reader," *New York World Telegram,* May 28, 1937, p. 19. Review of *Before I Forget.*

3. Maxwell Geismar, "Mr. Rascoe Returns to Memory Lane," *New York Times Book Review,* September 28, 1947, p. 3. Review of *We Were Interrupted.*

4. Edmund Wilson, "Burton Rascoe," *The New Republic,* LIX (May 29, 1929), 48. Review of *A Bookman's Daybook.*

5. Conrad Aiken, Letter, May 27, 1919.

6. Lewis Galantière, Letter, June 23, 1919.

7. Theodore Dreiser, Letter, May 10, 1919.

8. Alfred A. Knopf, Letter, April 7, 1919. Rascoe finished two of the introductions that year: *Madame Bovary* and *Manon Lescaut.* Of these introductions he told Cabell in a letter of October 20, 1919: "My preface to 'Bovary,' I take pride in, because of its prose rhythms and because I have said, I think, two new things about the book. The 'Manon' I kidded, which seemed to delight Knopf."

9. Hugh Walpole, Letter, April 20, 1920.

10. Vincent Starrett, "Burton Rascoe," typescript (BRC), n.d., but probably written in 1922.

11. Lewis Galantière, Letter, May 17, 1921.

12. Letter to Cabell, May 16, 1921.

13. Galantière, Letter, March 9, [1925?]. Written soon after Rascoe's "Day Book" column had stopped appearing in the *New York Herald Tribune* in 1924 and before Rascoe's first book, *Theodore Dreiser,* was published in 1925. Rascoe had given his reason in an earlier column for not compiling a book from his newspaper clippings: "F. P. Adams' 'Overset' I liked. He gains, I think, immensely in stature when read in book form. Usually the converse is true, especially when the book is made up of short items or paragraphs written for a daily paper. It is for that reason I find futile most books made up of reviews and criticisms originally published in magazines or newspapers. A conscience of this futility has restrained me when I have been urged by

publishers to bring together in a book the fugitive pieces I have written as a daily or weekly journalistic stint; but how many of them are worth reading twice? How few of such books are worth keeping on one's shelves?" ("Day Book," *New York Tribune Books,* October 11, 1922.)

14. Frank Moore Colby, Letter, January 9, 1922.

15. F. Scott Fitzgerald, Letter, n.d., but the rest of the letter suggests that it was written in the spring, probably in May, 1922. Rascoe had become literary editor of the *Tribune* on March 1, 1922.

16. Malcolm Cowley, Letter, March 23, 1923. Written at Giverny Par Vernon, Eure, France.

17. Isabel Patterson, "Burton Rascoe," *The Literary Spotlight,* edited by John Farrar (Garden City, New York, 1924), pp. 254–57.

18. Victor Llona, "La Littérature Française jugée . . . ," p. 9.

19. Llona, "Literary Paris," *Chicago Tribune,* March 1, 1925.

20. Galantière, Letter in Llona, "Literary Paris," March 1, 1925.

21. C. Hartley Grattan, Introduction to *A Bookman's Daybook* (ed. Grattan), by Burton Rascoe (New York, 1929), p. xii.

22. *Ibid.,* p. xiv.

23. Edmund Wilson, "Burton Rascoe," *The New Republic,* LIX (May 29, 1929), 49. All of Rascoe's books were reviewed in most of the newspapers, magazines, and journals throughout the country, and some were reviewed in England. Rascoe subscribed to a clipping service for many years and kept scrapbooks (BRC) of these clippings. I have tried in this chapter to compile representative comments from these many reviews that will reflect the different phases of Rascoe's critical reputation and reception.

24. "Books in Brief," *The Nation,* CXXVIII (April 24, 1929), 513.

25. Henry Hazlitt, "Four Critics: Eliot, Benda, Rascoe and Read," *New York Sun,* April 6, 1929, p. 12.

26. William Rose Benét, "*A Bookman's Daybook,*" *The Bookman,* LXIX (June, 1929), 440.

27. Malcolm Cowley, "The Conning Tower," *New York Herald Tribune,* June 8, 1934.

28. Carl Van Doren, Letter, October 11, 1932.

29. Lane Cooper, Letter, October 26, 1932.

30. William Soskin, "Reading and Writing," *New York Evening Post,* November 1, 1932, p. 11.

31. Lewis Gannett, "Books and Things," *New York Herald Tribune,* November 1, 1932.

32. William Lyon Phelps, "As I Like It," *Scribner's Magazine,* XCIII (April, 1933), 259.

33. J. Donald Adams, "With Bludgeon and Boomerang," *New York Times Book Review,* November 27, 1932, p. 2.

34. *Ibid.*

35. Murray Godwin, Letter, November 11, 1932.

36. Godwin, "The Heavies Weigh In," *The New Republic,* LXXIII (December 14, 1932), 134–35.

37. Alan Burton Clark, "Mr. Rascoe and Some Other Titans of Literature," *Richmond Times-Dispatch,* November 27, 1932, section III, p. 4.

38. C. Hartley Grattan, "Literary Sign-Posts," *Scribner's Magazine,* XCII (December, 1932), 7–8.

39. Donald A. Roberts and Edith Hamilton, "This Will Never Do," *The Saturday Review of Literature,* IX (December 31, 1932), 357–58, 360.

40. Ernest Boyd, "Literary Journalism," *The Nation,* CXXXVI (January 4, 1933), 22.

41. *Ibid.*

42. Archibald Henderson, "The Office Bookshelf," *Delta Sigma Nu Magazine,* March, 1933, pp. 395–96.

43. Bruce Catton, "Rascoe Discusses Literature Again," Newspaper Enterprise Association Service.

44. Howard Mumford Jones, "Rebellious Titans," *The Saturday Review of Literature,* X (December 9, 1933), 319.

45. "Of Making Many Books," *Philadelphia Public Ledger,* December 12, 1933. Clipping, BRC.

46. Fannie Butcher, "Rascoe Writes on Authors," *Chicago Tribune,* January 20, 1934, books sec., p. 8.

47. Sculley Bradley, "Rascoe Makes Literature a Living Subject," *Philadelphia Record,* December 17, 1933. Clipping, BRC.

48. Theodore Dreiser, Letter, May 4, 1934.

49. *The Bookman* had merged with and become *The American Review* in 1933.

50. L. B. Hessler, "On 'Bad Boy' Criticism," *The North American Review,* CCXL (September, 1935), 217.

51. *Ibid.*

52. Margaret Marshall and Mary McCarthy, "Our Critics, Right or Wrong: II. The Anti-Intellectuals," *The Nation,* CXLI (November 6, 1935), 542.

53. Presumably Van Doren and Krutch were included in Rascoe's group because they were both, at various times, members of the board of judges of The Literary Guild with Rascoe.

54. Marshall and McCarthy, p. 542.

55. Louis Paul, Letter, November 19, 1935.

56. George Macy, Letter, November 20, 1936.

57. Louis Paul, "Books and Mr. Rascoe," *Reading and Collecting: A Monthly Review of Rare and Recent Books,* I (May, 1937), 15.

58. *Ibid.*

59. "Bright Boy," *Time Magazine*, XXIX (May 31, 1937), 29.

60. John Chamberlain, "Eye Opener," *The New Republic*, LXXXXI (June 30, 1937), 229.

61. Harry Hansen, "Among the New Books," *Harper's Magazine*, CLXXV (July, 1937), n.p. Clipping, BRC.

62. Lloyd Morris, Review of *We Were Interrupted, New York Herald Tribune Books*, October 5, 1947, p. 1.

63. Lewis Gannett, Review of *We Were Interrupted, New York Herald Tribune Books*, December 12, 1947. Clipping, BRC.

64. James Gray, "Fun, All the Way," *The Saturday Review of Literature*, XXX (October 18, 1947), 13–14.

65. Two recent biographies making use of Rascoe material have been Arnold T. Schwab's *James Gibbons Huneker* (Stanford, 1963) and W. A. Swanberg's *Dreiser* (New York, 1965). No doubt others will follow.

66. Edmund Wilson, Letter, April 16.

Chapter Five

1. William Soskin "Burton Rascoe, from Mooncalf to Critic," *New York Herald Tribune Books*, May 30, 1937, p. 1.

2. "French Fiction for Americans; Notes and Comments," *Chicago Tribune*, March 15, 1919, books sec., p. 11.

3. Clipping (BRC) of "The Barnard Statue of the Drama," *Chicago Tribune*, n.d., but Drinkwater's play was printed in 1918.

4. Cf. the title of Rascoe's editorial with the title of James Russell Lowell's "On a Certain Condenscension Among Foreigners." The title, aim, and content of Lowell's essay indicate Rascoe's similar purpose.

5. *Before I Forget*, p. 398. First printed in the *Chicago Tribune* sometime during 1918–19 on Rascoe's Saturady page of Book News and Reviews. Another of these literary editorials, "Excuse the Glove," was also reprinted in *Before I Forget*, pp. 402–6.

6. *Ibid.*, p. 399.

7. "Day Book," *New York Tribune Books*, April 3. Clipping, BRC.

8. "Parisian Epilogue," in *A Bookman's Daybook*, p. 301. See Note 35 to Chapter II.

9. Letter to Louis Paul, July 20, 1936. In a letter to Paul a few days later (July 26), Rascoe said that ". . . for many years now I have been discovering new talent for publishers, getting books published for new authors and thereby making money for both authors and publishers. I could name you dozens of them—. . . . For all this I have never got a cent—not even gratitude." But just recently, he told Paul, Doubleday had hired him to scout for new talent.

10. Letter to Morris (?), November 6, 1932, BRC.
11. "Our Vicious Zeal," *Chicago Tribune*, n.d., books set. Clipping, BRC. Reprinted in *Before I Forget*, pp. 399–402. Rascoe's note: "This is one of several editorials I wrote against specific acts of censorship in general for the Saturday page ... during 1918–19, when censorship of literature by private organizations was rife."
12. *Ibid.*
13. *Ibid.*
14. Lewis Galantière, Letter, June 23, 1919.
15. Galantière, Letter, July 15, 1926.
16. Dreiser sent Rascoe copies of his correspondence with Paul Palmer, Sunday editor of the *New York World*, concerning the controversy over this article. Palmer's first letter to Dreiser was dated October 14, 1929.
17. Copy of letter from Dreiser to Rascoe (BRC), n.d.
18. Copy of letter to Dreiser (BRC), October 24, 1929.
19. Copy of letter to Palmer (BRC), October 25, 1929.
20. Theodore Dreiser, "Whom God Hath Joined Together ...," *Plain Talk*, VI (April, 1930), 401–4.
21. Rascoe's library (BRC).
22. Cabell, Letter, October 10, 1924.
23. Letter to Dreiser, June 16, 1931. Dreiser Collection.
24. Quoted by Rascoe in a marginal note on a clipping (BRC) of his *Esquire* article. See also "Poet Sues Durante," *Newsweek*, III (March 31, 1934), 34.
25. Alfred Kreymborg, Letter, August 23, 1934. Written at Peterboro, New Hampshire.
26. Kreymborg, Letter, October 21, 1934.
27. Galantière, Letter, April 10, [?].
28. *Fanfare*, pamphlet on H. L. Mencken (New York, 1920).
29. "The Court of Books with Its Nobles, Knaves and Fools," *Plain Talk*, V (December, 1929), 754.
30. "The Daybook," *New York American*, March 12, 1931, p. 17.
31. Louis Paul, Letter, October 15, 1934.
32. "A Bookman's Daybook," *New York Herald Tribune Books*, June 15, 1924. This entry was reprinted as "Ellis, Whitehead and Hemingway" in *A Bookman's Daybook*, pp. 253–54.
33. Ernest Hemingway, Letter to Edmund Wilson—quoted by Wilson in *A Literary Chronicle: 1920–1950* (Garden City, New York, 1956), p. 41.
34. *Ibid.*, p. 48.
35. Malcolm Cowley, *Exile's Return* (New York, 1951), pp. 176–77.
36. Cowley, *After the Genteel Tradition* (New York, 1937), p. 245.

37. "A Bookman's Daybook," *New York Tribune Books*, August 20, 1922.

38. *Ibid.*, October 14, 1922. Reprinted as "The Case of Gertrude Stein" in *A Bookman's Daybook*, pp. 42–43.

39. *Ibid.*, March 6, 1924, p. 22.

40. "A Bookman's Daybook," *New York Sun*, July 16, 1932, p. 16.

41. *Ibid.*, July 9, 1932, p. 4.

42. Clipping (BRC) of "A Bookman's Daybook," *New York Sun*, n.d., but *Expression in America* was published in 1932.

43. "A Bookman's Daybook," *New York Sun*, September 16, 1932, p. 29.

44. "Among the New Books," *Arts and Decoration*, May, 1930, p. 110. Review of Joseph Hergesheimer's *The Party Dress*. Clipping, BRC.

45. *We Were Interrupted*, pp. 155–56.

46. Perry Miller, Review of a paperback edition of *Jurgen: A Comedy of Justice*, *New York Herald Tribune Books*, February 11, 1962, p. 12.

47. Letter to Cabell, October 6, 1930. Rascoe often stated his desire to give up editorial work. For example, he wrote to Louis Paul on January 25, 1938, that he had resigned from the Literary Guild in May, 1937, because "I wanted to break away from the editorial grind and give more time to writing." And he wrote to Paul on September 19, 1938, that "The example of John Steinbeck, and to a degree your own, which is the unheeded example long ago set me by Dreiser and Cabell, has strengthened me in my forty-fifth year in a definite resolve no longer to scatter my shots and dissipate my energies by being an editor four-fifths of the time and a writer of books one-fifth of the time, the one-fifth largely at the expense of sleep and recreation."

48. *We Were Interrupted*, p. 155.

49. In his unpublished typescript, "Chicago's Gold Age in Life and Letters," Rascoe in 1956 attempted to refute what he said are distortions of the historical literary record by Ben Hecht, Henry B. Sell, and Mencken. First, he said his book pages in the *Chicago Tribune* antedated Sell's in the *Chicago Daily News* by over three years—1916–1919—and that Sell's was an imitation of his, not the other way around, as Hecht, in *A Child of the Century* (1954) had said (pp. 341–42). Second, Rascoe said that he had been responsible for the literary excitement that caused Mencken to say that Chicago was the literary capital of the United States. Mencken later, Rascoe said, tried to conceal this when he revised his *Baltimore Evening Sun* article for *The Smart Set* by extracting Rascoe's name twice from the text which he did not otherwise revise, and by claiming that he had "discovered" Cabell as far back as 1909. This was absolutely unfounded, Rascoe

wrote. Furthermore, Mencken only mentioned Rascoe's name in print twice—and Rascoe was the critic who first—by two years—wrote an article of length, substance and enthusiasm, treating Mencken seriously as a literary figure and force in American letters. Rascoe also said in this typescript that he was the first writer, in Chicago or elsewhere, to write extensively of Sherwood Anderson as a new and original prodigy in American fiction and also the first and almost the only book critic, or reviewer, to greet Hecht's first novel, *Erik Dorn*, with a sympathetic and perceptive, lengthy appraisal ("An American Epithetician," *The Bookman*, October, 1921); this review, Rascoe said, antedated by two years the next extensive notice of Hecht—Harry Hansen's in *Midwest Portraits* (1923).

Selected Bibliography

PRIMARY SOURCES

1. Books and Contributions to Books by Rascoe

Books

Theodore Dreiser. New York: McBride, 1925.
A Bookman's Daybook. Edited with an Introduction by C. Hartley Grattan. New York: Liveright, 1929.
Titans of Literature. New York: Putnam's, 1932. Reprinted as *Story of the World's Greatest Writers.* New York: Blue Ribbon Books, 1935.
Prometheans. New York: Putnam's, 1933.
Before I Forget. Garden City: Doubleday, Doran, 1937.
The Joys of Reading: Life's Greatest Pleasure. Garden City: Doubleday, Doran, 1937.
Bell Starr: "The Bandit Queen". New York: Random House, 1941
We Were Interrupted. Garden City: Doubleday, 1947.

Introductions

Madam Bovary. Gustave Flaubert. New York: Knopf, 1919.
Manon Lescaut. Abbé Prévost. New York: Knopf, 1919.
Mademoiselle de Maupin. Théophile Gautier. New York: Knopf, 1920.
Erik Dorn. Ben Hecht. New York: Modern Library, 1921.
Nana. Emile Zola, New York: Knopf, 1922.
Chivalry. James Branch Cabell. New York: Modern Library, 1922.
The Triumph of Death. Gabrielle D'Annunzio. New York: Modern Library, 1923.
Tricks of Women and Other Armenian Tales. Compiled and translated by P. F. Cooper. New York: William Morrow, 1928.
A High Wind in Jamaica. Richard Hughes. New York: Harper, 1930.
Floyd Gibbons, Night of the Air. Douglas Gilbert. New York: McBride, 1930.
The Decameron. Boccaccio. New York: Limited Editions Club, 1930.
Boom in Paradise. Theyre H. Weigall. New York: Alfred H. King, 1932.
The Natural Philosophy of Love. Rémy de Gourmont, translated by Ezra Pound. New York: Liveright, 1932.
Extra! Extra! Deadlines and Josslyn. Henry Justin Smith. Chicago: Sterling North, 1933.

The Memoirs of Vincent Nolte. New York: G. Howard Watt, 1934.
The Great Trek. Max Miller. New York: Doubleday, Doran, 1935.
The Ballad of Reading Gaol. Oscar Wilde. New York Limited Editions Club, 1937.
Sister Carrie. Theodore Dreiser. New York: Limited Editions Club, 1939.

Collaborations

Fanfare. Pamphlet on H. L. Mencken. Rascoe contributed the title essay. New York: Knopf, 1920.
The Literary Spotlight. Edited by John C. Farrar. Contributed anonymous personal sketches of H. L. Mencken, Joseph Hergesheimer, Sherwood Anderson, John Farrar, Henry Blake Fuller. Garden City: George H. Doran, 1924. The Mencken sketch originally appeared in *The Bookman* of Febrruay, 1922, pp. 551–54, and was reprinted in *Before I Forget,* pp. 438–42. The sketches of Hergesheimer and Anderson were also reprinted in *Before I Forget,* Appendix IX.
The Bookman Anthology of Essays. Edited by John C. Farrar. Contributed an essay on George Santayana. New York: George H. Doran, 1924.
These United States: A Symposium. Edited by Ernest Gruening. Second Series. Contributed "Oklahoma: Low Jacks and the Crooked Game." New York: Boni and Liveright, 1924. Originally: "Oklahoma," *The Nation,* CXVII (July 11, 1923), 34–37.
The American Caravan. Edited by Alfred Kreymborg, Lewis Mumford, and Paul Rosenfeld. Contributed an interior monologue, "What Is Love?" from *Gustibus,* an autobiographical novel he was then writing but which he never finished. New York: Macauley, 1928.
Morrow's Almanack for 1928. Edited by Burton Rascoe. Wrote bogus horoscopes and compiled the calendars. New York: William Morrow, 1928.
Morrow's Almanack for 1929. Edited by Burton Rascoe. Wrote bogus horoscopes and compiled the calendars. New York: William Morrow, 1929.
Morrow's Almanack for 1930. Edited by Tiffany Thayer. Rascoe wrote short essays for each month of the year. New York: William Morrow, 1930.
The Critique of Humanism: A Symposium. Edited by C. Hartley Grattan. Contributed "Pupils of Polonius," satirizing the New Humanist movement. New York: Harcourt, Brace, 1930.

Selected Bibliography

Essay Annual for 1933. Edited by Erich A. Walter. Contributed an essay on Montaigne, from *Titans of Literature.* Chicago: Scott, Foresman, 1933.

Spoofs. Edited by Richard B. Glaenzer. Contributed a burlesque of bankers, brokers, and financiers. New York: McBride, 1933.

Modern American Prose. Edited by Carl Van Doren. Contributed an essay on Lucian, from *Prometheans.* New York: Harcourt, Brace, 1934.

The Smart Set Anthology. Edited by Burton Rascoe and Groff Conklin. Rascoe wrote the Introduction, a history of *The Smart Set,* and contributed the short story, "Caste." New York: Reynal and Hitchcock, 1934.

American Literature. Edited by Henry Garland Bennett. Contributed the essay "What Are Intellectuals?" New York: American Book Company, 1935.

The New Republic Anthology. Edited by Groff Conklin. Contributed "The Grim Anniversary," an account of the panic of October, 1929. New York: Dodge, 1936.

An American Reader. Edited by Burton Rascoe. Wrote the Introduction, a history of publishing in America, and an introductory essay for each of the divisions of the anthology. New York: Putnam's, 1938.

The Patriotic Anthology. Edited by Barbara Moses Olds with an Introduction by Carl Van Doren. Contributed the essay "Self-Evident Truths." New York: Doubleday, Doran, 1941.

The Americana Annual. Edited by A. H. Dannald and others. Contributed articles on American literature and book publishing in 1946. Chicago: Americana Corporation, 1947.

10 Eventful Years. Edited by Walter Yust. Contributed the article "Tendencies in the U. S. Drama" (between 1937 and 1946). Vol. IV. Chicago: Encyclopedia Britannica, 1947.

The Americana Annual. Edited by A. H. Dannald and others. Contributed articles on American literature and book publishing in 1947. Chicago: Americana Corporation, 1948.

Painted Veils. James G. Huneker. Contributed "A Note About Painted Veils." New York: Avon Publications, 1954.

2. Representative Articles and Essays in Newspapers and Magazines by Rascoe

This bibliography does not list any items from the following newspaper columns unless reprinted in one of Rascoe's books: "A Bookman's Day Book" in the *New York Tribune* (and *Herald Tribune*), 1922–1924; syndicated newspaper column, "A Daybook of a New

Yorker," 1925–1927; dramatic criticism in the *New York World-Telegram*, 1942–1946; syndicated newspaper column, "TV First-Nighter," 1954–1957.

"Personal Ethics Without Sweetmeats," *Chicago Tribune*, April 1, 1916, books sec., p. 9. Review of Willard Huntington Wright's novel, *The Man of Promise*.

Diary Entry, May 20, 1917, Rascoe Collection. Quoted in *Before I Forget*, pp. 342–45. Describes Rascoe's feelings at the time of the entry of the United States into World War I.

"Fanfare," *Chicago Tribune*, November 11, 1917, books sec., p. 7. First lengthy critical treatment of Mencken anywhere.

"Here's A Chance to Own Another First Edition," *Chicago Tribune*, December 29, 1917, books sec., p. 9. Review of James Branch Cabell's *The Cream of the Jest*—Rascoe's first review of a book by Cabell.

"Prof. Sherman Gives Asylum to His Brood," *Chicago Tribune*, January 12, 1918. Satirical review of Stuart P. Sherman's *On Contemporary Literature*. Reprinted in *Before I Forget*, pp. 407–8.

"On a Certain Condescension Among Our Natives," *Chicago Tribune*, February 16, 1918, books sec., p. 9. Reprinted in *Before I Forget*, pp. 396–99.

"Conrad Aiken's 'The Charnel Rose,'" *Chicago Tribune*, December 28, 1918, books sec., p. 7.

"French Fiction for Americans; Notes and Comments," *Chicago Tribune*, March 15, 1919, books sec., p. 11. Attacks Edgar Jepson and "insular" English critics.

"We've Had About Enough of Ezra; Note on Kreymborg," *Chicago Tribune*, March 29, 1919, books sec., p. 13.

"Dreiser Shakes the Potter's Hand," *Chicago Tribune*, October 11, 1919, books sec., p. 13. Essay on Dreiser's *The Hand of the Potter*.

"Aiken's 'Scepticism,'" *Chicago Tribune*, January 31, 1920, books sec., p. 13. Attacks Aiken as a critic but praises him as a poet.

"An American Epithetician," *The Bookman*, LIV (October, 1921), 163, 165, 166. Review of *Erik Dorn*, by Ben Hecht. Reprinted as Introduction to *Erik Dorn* (New York: Modern Library, 1921).

"The Motion Pictures: An Industry, Not an Art," *The Bookman*, LIV (November, 1921), 193–99.

"Notes for an Epitaph: H. L. Mencken," *New York Evening Post*, Literary Review, March 4, 1922, p. 461 (front page). Rascoe sees Mencken's importance as a literary force at an end.

"The Biblical Style," *The New Republic*, XXX (May 17, 1922), 338–39. Used in *Titans* in "Milton the Conscience," pp. 277–79.

"Art and Clive Bell," *The Reviewer*, III (June, 1922), 487–95.

"A Residue of Reading," *New York Tribune Books*, September 3, 1922, p. 7. Attacks *This Freedom*, by A. S. M. Hutchinson.

"Mr. Hecht's 'Gargoyles,'" *New York Tribune Books*, September 24, 1922, p. 7.

"The Dead Give-Away," *New York Tribune Books*, September 24, 1922, p. 8. Reprinted in *A Bookman's Daybook*, pp. 3–11. Rascoe discusses his critical theories and literary tastes.

"The Bible of the Nineties," *New York Tribune Books*, October 8, 1922, p. 7. Review of *A Rebours*, by J. K. Huysmans.

"The Sad Case of Stuart P. Sherman," *New York Tribune Books*, December 17, 1922, p. 17. Review of Sherman's *Americans*.

"In the Waste Land with Mr. Zane Grey," *New York Tribune Books*, January 21, 1923, p. 19. Attacks *Wanderer of the Waste Land*, by Zane Grey.

"Joseph Conrad Comes to See Us, Not to Chide or 'Uplift,'" *New York Tribune Books*, May 2, 1923, pp. 1, 6. Reprinted in *A Bookman's Daybook*, pp. 105–11.

"America Is Beginning to Inspire European Art," *Arts and Decoration*, XX (January, 1924), 18.

"Carl Sandburg," *New York Evening Post*, Literary Review, September 27, 1924, pp. 1–2. One of the first extensive studies of Sandburg the man and poet. Reprinted in *Before I Forget*, pp. 434–38.

"Contemporary Reminiscences," *Arts and Decoration*, XXII (March, 1925), 38, 70, 75. Contains portrait of E. E. Cummings in Paris in the fall of 1924. Reprinted in *A Bookman's Daybook*, pp. 297–305, as "Parisian Epilogue."

"Mencken, Dreiser, Scott Fitzgerald, Van Vechten, Ernest Boyd Were There But the Lit'ry Party Was a FLOP!" in Rascoe's syndicated column, "The Daybook of a New Yorker," June 23, 1926. Reprinted in *We Were Interrupted*, pp. 299–302.

"A Salute to Youth," *The Daily Maroon*, University of Chicago, Celebrities Number, 1927, pp. 11, 20.

"A New Master," *The Bookman*, LXVI (January, 1928), 559–62. Reviews Thornton Wilder's *The Bridge of San Luis Rey* as a "classic."

"'Criticobiografiction,'" *The New Republic*, LX (October 9, 1929), Pt. 2, 211–13. Review satirizing George Jean Nathan's style in *Monks Are Monks*.

"The Court of Books with Its Nobles, Knaves and Fools," *Plain Talk*, V (December, 1929), 754. Contains Rascoe's laudatory comments on Graham Greene's first novel, *The Man Within*.

"Life of a Critic," *Plain Talk*, VI (January, 1930), 111–19. Review attacking *The Life and Letters of Stuart P. Sherman*, by Jacob Zeitlin and Homer Woodbridge.

"The New Humanists," *New York World,* April 20, 1930, books sec., pp. 1, 6.

"Humanism and America," *Plain Talk,* VI (April, 1930), 491–98. Review attacking *Humanism and America* (ed. Norman Foerster).

"The Grim Anniversary: Irresponsible Reminiscences of the Hoover Panic," *The New Republic,* LXIV (October 29, 1930), 285–88. Reprinted in *The New Republic Anthology* (ed. Groff Conklin), and in *We Were Interrupted,* pp. 331–42.

"At the Bier of Symbolism," *New York Herald Tribune Books,* March 1, 1931, p. 7. Review of Edmund Wilson's *Axel's Castle.*

"A Weak Will to Power," *New York Herald Tribune Books,* March 13, 1932, p. 4. Review of Oswald Spengler's *Man and Technics.* Labels Spengler "a Junker defeatist" and attacks his philosophic ideas.

"A Bookman's Daybook," *New York Sun,* May 7, 1932, p. 8. Review of Edmund Wilson's *The American Jitters.*

"A Bookman's Daybook," *New York Sun,* May 17, 1932, p. 25. Review of William Harlan Hale's *Challenge to Defeat.*

"Rascoe's Riposte," *New York Sun,* June 11, 1932, p. 36. Letter answering Ezra Pound's charge that Rascoe had lied (in an earlier *Sun* column) about being one of the first critics to mention Hemingway's work.

"A Bookman's Daybook," *New York Sun,* July 9, 1932, p. 4, and July 16, 1932, p. 16. Attacks Grant C. Knight's *American Literature and Culture* and defends James G. Huneker.

"Pain and Beauty of Life," *New York Herald Tribune Books,* March 10, 1935, p. 1. Review of Thomas Wolfe's *Of Time and the River.*

"A Novel that Makes You Feel Good," *New York Herald Tribune Books,* October 27, 1935, p. 3. Review of Barry Benefield's *Valiant Is the Word for Carrie.*

"Esquire's Five Minute Shelf," *Esquire,* VII (January, 1937), 101, 203–4. On Rascoe's son's suicide.

"Reflections on the Aim and Intention of 'Before I Forget,'" *Wings* (June, 1937), pp. 5–8. Reprinted in *Before I Forget,* pp. ix–xii.

"Self-Confidential," *The Saturday Review of Literature,* XVII (December 4, 1937), 11. Review parodying Gertrude Stein's *Everybody's Autobiography.*

"'Scholars' Mugg the Camera," *Newsweek,* XI (April 25, 1938), 30. Review of Lloyd Eschleman's *Moulders of Destiny.*

"Mencken, Nathan and Cabell," *The American Mercury,* XLIX (March, 1940), 362–68. Says new books by these three older writers show that they can write; the younger writers cannot.

"Negro Novel and White Reviewers," *The American Mercury,* L (May,

1940), 113–17. Attacks "social significance" in Richard Wright's *Native Son*.

"Wolfe, Farrell and Hemingway," *The American Mercury*, LI (December, 1940), 493–98. Says Wolfe (before he died) and Farrell achieved maturity; Hemingway had not.

SECONDARY SOURCES

ADAMS, J. DONALD. "With Bludgeon and Boomerang," *New York Times Book Review*, November 27, 1932, p. 2. Review of *Titans*. One of the best analyses of a work by Rascoe; compares *Titans* to Will Durant's *The Story of Philosophy*.

BENÉT, WILLIAM ROSE. "A Bookman's Daybook," *The Bookman*, LXIX (June, 1929), 440–41. Review of *Daybook*. A good description of the qualities of Rascoe's "Daybook" column, which Benét felt was the best of its kind to ever appear in an American newspaper.

BOYD, ERNEST. "Literary Journalism," *The Nation*, CXXXVI (January 4, 1933), 22. Review of *Titans*. Long defense of Rascoe's superb literary journalism.

BUTCHER, FANNY. "Rascoe Writes on Authors," *Chicago Tribune*, January 30, 1934, books sec., p. 8. Review of *Prometheans*. Accurately judges *Prometheans* to be inferior to *Titans* in both form and matter.

CHAMBERLAIN, JOHN. "Eye Opener," *The New Republic*, XXIX (May 31, 1937), 228–29. Review of *Before I Forget*. Fair evaluation of Rascoe's contributions to America's literary awakening.

CLEATON, IRENE and ALLEN. *Books and Battles, American Literature: 1920–1930*. Boston: Houghton Mifflin, 1937. Puts Rascoe in the mainstream of the radical literary developments of the 1920's.

COLUM, PADRAIC and CABELL, MARGARET FREEMAN, eds. *Between Friends: Letters of James Branch Cabell and Others*. Introduction by Carl Van Vechten. New York: Harcourt, Brace and World, 1962. Contains some of Rascoe's correspondence with Cabell.

COWLEY, MALCOLM. *Exile's Return: A Literary Odyssey of the 1920's*. New York: The Viking Press, rev. ed., 1951. Says that Rascoe's "Day Book" "gave a better picture of that frenzied age than any historian could hope to equal" (176).

DUFFEY BERNARD. *The Chicago Renaissance in American Letters: A Crictical History*. East Lansing: The Michigan State University Press, 1954. Concludes that Rascoe's book pages in the *Chicago Tribune* from 1917 until 1920 were conducted with "considerable liveliness and intelligence" and that "more strictly perhaps than any of his contemporaries, Rascoe argued the cause and forwarded the accomplishments of the early Liberation." Praises Rascoe for opening "full the gates of the *Tribune* to Chicago's renaissance" (257).

EATON, G. D. "A Lusty Howl from Tomb," *New York Morning Telegraph,* August 16, 1925, p. 7. Review of *Theodore Dreiser.* An appraisal of Rascoe's pioneer critical work, and of *Theodore Dreiser.* Sees Rascoe as one of the best critics in America.

GEISMAR, MAXWELL. "Mr. Rascoe Returns to Memory Lane," *New York Times Book Review,* September 28, 1947, pp. 3, 33. Review of *We Were Interrupted.* Says that Rascoe was a central figure in the Chicago literary movement, and that at times "he seemed to be the movement."

GRAY, JAMES. "Fun, All the Way," *The Saturday Review,* XXX (October 18, 1947), 13–14. Review of *We Were Interrupted.* Sees Rascoe as the "essential twentieth-century American" in the field of letters.

HAMILTON, EDITH and ROBERTS, DONALD A. "This Will Never Do," *The Saturday Review of Literature,* IX (December 31, 1932), 357–58, 360. Letters to the editor attacking *Titans.* Miss Hamilton has reprinted her letter in *The Ever-Present Past.* New York: W. W. Norton, 1964.

HESSLER, L. B. "On 'Bad Boy' Criticism," *The North American Review,* CCXL (September, 1935), 214–24. Attacks Rascoe's method of subjective criticism.

KAZIN, ALFRED. *Our Native Grounds.* New York: Reynal and Hitchcock, 1942. Recognizes the "gusto," "courage," "enthusiasm" in Rascoe's Chicago literary work, and its importance in freeing American literature, but says it amounts to no more than this.

LLONA, VICTOR. "La Littérature française jugée par les grands écrivains étrangers Burton Rascoe," *Le Journal Littéraire,* January 31, 1925, p. 9. Rascoe gives his views on contemporary French literature in Paris in 1924.

MARSHALL, MARGARET and McCARTHY, MARY. "Our Critics, Right or Wrong: II. The Anti-Intellectuals," *The Nation,* CXLI (November 6, 1935), 542–44. Accuses Rascoe of heading a group of anti-intellectual critics.

[PATTERSON, ISABEL]. "Burton Rascoe," in *The Literary Spotlight,* edited by John C. Farrar. New York: George H. Doran, 1924. Portrait of Rascoe the man, journalist, and critic by Rascoe's assistant for two years on the *New York Tribune.*

PAUL, LOUIS. "Books and Mr. Rascoe," *Reading and Collecting: A Monthly Review of Rare and Recent Books,* I (May, 1937), 15, 29. An estimate of Rascoe's critical ability by a writer whom Rascoe had encouraged and a friend.

Selected Bibliography

POUND, EZRA. "Pound to Rascoe," *New York Sun,* June 11, 1932, p. 36.
Letter accusing Rascoe of lying about being one of the earliest
critics to mention Hemingway's work.

SOSKIN, WILLIAM. "Burton Rascoe, from Mooncalf to Critic," *New
York Herald Tribune Books,* May 30, 1937, p. 1. Review of *Before
I Forget.* Good appraisal of the importance of Rascoe's early work.

WILSON, EDMUND. "The All-Star Literary Vaudeville," *The New Republic,* XXXXVII (June 30, 1926), 158–63. Reprinted in *A Literary Chronicle: 1920–1950.* Garden City: Doubleday Anchor, 1956.
Wilson writes that "Burton Rascoe has performed the astonishing
and probably unprecedented feat of making literature into news"
(83).

———. "Burton Rascoe," *The New Republic,* LIX (May 29, 1929),
49. Review of *A Bookman's Daybook.* Reprinted in *The Shores
of Light: A Literary Chronicle of the Twenties and Thirties.* New
York: Farrar, Strauss, and Young, 1952. Early estimate of Rascoe's
critical abilities and some analysis of his work by a major critic.

Index

Brownell, William C., 68
Browning, Robert, 72
Brunetière, Vincent de Paul, 67
Buchanan, Charles, 53, 54, 133*n*
Burke, Kenneth, 54-55
Burton, Harry Payne, 25, 28
Butcher, Fanny, 77, 99

Cabell, James Branch, 24, 27, 28, 30,
    31, 33, 36, 38, 39, 40, 46, 59, 60,
    64, 65, 67, 72, 84, 85, 86, 90, 99,
    104, 105, 107, 108, 110, 113, 123,
    124, 125, 126, 127, 135*n*, 143*n*
Caesar, 44, 56, 97
Caldwell, Erskine, 36
Calverton, V. F., 122
Carco, Francis, 61
Carlyle, Thomas, 44
Cather, Willa, 77, 126
Catton, Bruce, 99
Catullus, 97
Cézanne, Paul, 119, 122
Chamberlain, John, 104, 125
Charlemagne, 46
Chekhov, Anton, 24, 47
Chicago, Daily News, 60
"Chicago's Golden Age in Life and
    Letters" (Rascoe typescript), 76,
    143-44*n*
Chicago Sun, 38
Chicago Tribune, 21, 22, 23, 25, 26,
    60, 66, 69, 70, 82, 84, 85, 87, 88,
    99, 107, 110, 124, 143*n*
Child of the Century, A (Hecht),
    143*n*
Chopin, (Huneker), 121
Chopin, Frédéric, 121
Christian Scientists, 25
Christy, H. C., 11, 122
Churchill, Winston, 125
Cicero, 97
Clarke, Alan Burton, 94-95
Classic Features Syndicate, 40
Coblentz, Stanton, 26
Cohn, Louis Henry, 117
Colby, Frank More, 87
Coleridge, Samuel Taylor, 56
Colet, Mme Louise, 62
Collins, Seward, 30, 31, 80

Congreve, William, 65
Conklin, Groff, 33
"Conning Tower, The," (F. P. Adams'
    column), 84
Conrad, Joseph, 43, 47, 108
Contemporary Literature, On (Sher-
    man), 58-60, 70, 79
Cooke, Alastair, 136-37*n*
Cooper, Lane, 92
Corbière, Tristan, 28, 78, 82
Corelli, Marie, 125
Cowley, Malcolm, 87, 91, 118
Cream of the Jest, The (Cabell), 64,
    87, 124
Critique of Humanism (ed. Grattan),
    81, 82
Cummings, E. E., 28, 31, 56, 57, 109,
    110
Cuppy, Will, 26

Dadaists, 61
D'Annunzio, Gabriele, 122
Dante, 78, 81, 93, 94, 98, 101
Das Kapital (Marx), 32
Daudet, Alphonse, 111
"Day Book" (Rascoe), 26, 27, 48, 53,
    77, 78, 83, 87, 88, 89, 92, 115, 116,
    117, 118, 119
Day, Clarence 56
Decadence, 61
*Decline and Fall of the Roman Em-
    pire* (Gibbon), 47
Dekker, Thomas, 61
Detroit Athletic Club News, 39
De Voto, Bernard, 123, 124
Dial, The, 77, 117
Dickens, Charles, 98
Divine Comedy (Dante), 68
Dostoievsky, Fyodor, 47, 48, 71, 115
Doubleday, Doran & Co., 33, 34, 39,
    110, 141*n*
Doubleday, Russell, 34
Double-Dealer, The, 26
Douglas, A. Donald, 26
Dreiser (Swanberg), 129*n*
Dreiser, Theodore, 24, 29, 31, 46, 49-
    50, 59, 66, 79, 84, 85, 89, 99, 100,
    105, 108, 110, 112, 114, 118, 120,
    125, 126, 143*n*

Index

Peattie, Robert Burns, 22
Peter Middleton (Marks), 53
Petronius, 46, 78, 97, 99, 100
Phelps, William Lyon, 45, 92-93, 102
Philadelphia Public Ledger, 99
Philadelphia Record, 99
Phillipe, Charles-Louis, 24
Plagued by the Nightingale (Boyle), 115
Plain Talk, 31, 59, 81, 113, 115
Plautus, 56
Plutarch, 44
Poe, Edgar Allan, 82
Poetry, 107
Pollard, Percival, 72
Porter, Eleanor H., 77, 125
Porter, Gene Stratton, 125
"Portrait of a Woman" (Dreiser), 31
Pound, Ezra, 78, 82, 83, 107, 110
Prejudices (Mencken), 74, 75, 87
Preston, Keith, 31, 65
Prometheans, Ancient and Modern (Rascoe), 32-33, 45, 46, 98, 99, 100
Propaganda for War, 1914-1917 (Peterson), 35
Propertius, Sextus, 97
Proust, Marcel, 24, 82, 84, 95
"Pupils of Polonius" (Rascoe), 81

Quiller-Couch, Sir Arthur, 56
Quintilian, 56

Rabelais, François, 55, 95, 11
Rascoe, Burton:
  Fulton, Kentucky, Shawnee, Oklahoma, 19; high school, early writing attempts, 20-21; early reading and studies, 20; first newspaper column in *Shawnee Herald,* 21; at the University of Chicago, 21; newspaper work, 21-22; fired by *Chicago Tribune,* 25; resumes newspaper work in Chicago, 25; goes to *McCall's* in New York as an editor, 25; becomes literary editor of *New York Tribune,* 26; starts "Day Book" column, 26-27; fired by *New York Tribune,* 27;

  goes to Paris, 28; writes syndicated column in New York, 29; becomes editor of *The Bookman,* 30; writes another "Day Book" column, 32; becomes literary critic for *Esquire,* 33; on editorial board of The Literary Guild of America, 33; edits *Smart Set Anthology,* 33; writes autobiography, *Before I Forget* (*q.v.*), 33; sued by Max Annenberg, 33; quits *Esquire,* 34; writes for *Newsweek* and *American Mercury,* 34, 36-37; argues with Van Wyck Brooks, 37; becomes director of amateur theatricals at Adelphi College, 39; writes syndicated column reviewing television shows, 40; death, 40; *see also* Chronology *and* Contents
Rascoe, Elizabeth Burton, 19-20
Rascoe, Matthew Lafayette, 19-20
Rascoe, Mrs. Hazel, 106
Read, Herbert, 90
Real Detective Stories, 40
Redman, Ben Ray, 26
"Reflections on the Aim and Intention of *Before I Forget*" (Rascoe), 41
Reidy, Tom, 60
Remembrance of Things Past (Proust), 24
Rice, Elmer, 109
Rimbaud, Arthur, 28
Riquarius (Richard Atwater), 65
Roberts, Donald A., 34, 35, 96, 100
Robinson, Edwin Arlington, 72
Roosevelt, Nicholas, 26
Rubáiyát, 122

Sainte-Beuve, Charles, 54, 56, 65
"Saint Mark" (Rascoe), 46, 99, 100
Sandburg, Carl, 26, 57-58, 61, 107
Santayana, George, 26
Sarcoë, Boturn (Burton Rascoe anagram), 134n
Sarett, Lew, 58
Saturday Review of Literature, The, 35, 82, 96, 99, 105
Satyricon (Petronius), 78